MEXICAN-AMERICANS
IN THE SOUTHWEST

D0868972

MEXICAN-AMERICANS
IN THE SOUTHWEST

by

ERNESTO GALARZA
HERMAN GALLEGOS
JULIAN SAMORA

Photographs by George Ballis

PUBLISHED IN COOPERATION WITH THE
ANTI-DEFAMATION LEAGUE OF B'NAI B'RITH

McNally & Loftin, Publishers
Santa Barbara

Library of Congress Catalog Card Number: 77-100639

Manufactured in the United States of America by
Kimberly Press, Inc., Goleta, California

Published through the courtesy of the Ford Foundation, sponsor of the two-year study on which this book—in the form of a report submitted to the Ford Foundation in December, 1966—is based. The opinions expressed in the report do not necessarily represent the views of the Foundation.

The work presented or reported herein was published pursuant to a Grant from the U.S. Office of Education, Department of Health, Education, and Welfare. However, the opinions expressed herein do not necessarily reflect the position or policy of the U.S. Office of Education, and no official endorsement by the U.S. Office of Education should be inferred.

CONTENTS

INTRODUCTION

The people of this study are as old as the Spanish con-
quests of the 1500's before there was a British Jamestown
and as recent as tomorrow's immigrant who will walk
across the border, visa in hand, to join relatives in East
Los Angeles or Denver.

They are as rural and rooted as a mountain villager of
Trampas, New Mexico, and as mobile and urban as a
United States congressman.

Their early ancestors contributed to the area, and con-
sequently to American culture, the domesticated animals
of the region: horses, cattle, sheep, and goats. They brought
the fruits and most of the vegetables that have made agri-
business what it is in the Southwest today. They brought
the knowledge and the means to extract the minerals of
the earth. The livestock industry and its concomitant cow-
boy mystique are their legacy. Irrigation and present-day
water laws derive from them. Christianity came with them.

Some say they were greedy and undoubtedly many were;
but many spent their fortunes for the sake of colonization.
Their treatment of the Indians was harsh and exploitative,
but as often as not the Indian was incorporated into the
society (even through marriage), rather than killed, driven

off, or corralled in reservations. Racism was not one of their contributions to this land.

Later ancestors, colonists of a different type, brought to a newly-unified country the brawn and muscle needed for its development. They were poor and they lacked sophisticated skills. Yet they built the railroads, not only in the Southwest but in the North and East. Their sweat developed the vast agricultural lands. They plowed the land, planted the seed, and produced the harvest. Their labor constructed the houses and public buildings. They cut the timber and built the highways. And out of ground that had once been theirs, they created the West—for the use, profit, and enjoyment of others.

The descendants of these heterogeneous groups are now commonly known as Mexican-Americans. The great majority reside in the Southwest, and the rest—some 15 to 20 percent—are concentrated in such midwestern and eastern urban centers as Kansas City, Chicago Heights, the South Chicago-East Chicago-Gary complex, Lansing, Saginaw, Detroit, Toledo, and Washington, D.C.

Over a two-year period of study, the three authors traveled through most of the United States and parts of Mexico. We sought out the Mexican-American in his diverse settings and circumstances, and observed at first hand the factors influencing him.

On the Mexican side of the border we saw cities teeming with poor and unemployed people, waiting for a chance to cross the border into the United States.

In the early morning on the international bridge into El Paso, one can see thousands upon thousands of Mexican workers commuting to their jobs in the United States. In the evening they will return to Ciudad Juarez with bags of goods purchased in the United States. There is mutual benefit to the two countries in this process: for Mexico it is the employment of its people and the dollars brought back; for the United States it is the low wages paid and the money left behind in return for American merchandise. At the same time, however, these commuters are depressing wages, taking away jobs from American citizens, thwarting American labor's efforts to organize, and pushing the less well off American citizen (the Mexican-American) on to the never-ending stream of agricultural migratory labor in search of jobs and better wages. These workday shuttlings may be observed at all entry points along the border, and coupled with the daily crossings of people coming into the United States for shopping or pleasure, they profoundly affect the entire region.

At the border—as well as in cities throughout the United States—one also finds the wetback, who will cross illegally and depress wages even more than the commuter does. Because they create unfair competition for available jobs, the wetback and the commuter are resented by the Mexican-Americans, particularly those living near the border.

In the barrios of San Antonio and Houston, the *colonias* of Los Angeles and Albuquerque—wherever we went—we heard about lack of housing, lack of jobs, and discrimination in employment at all levels above the most menial and lowest paid. People told us about inadequate schools, irrelevant curricula, uninterested educators, and the accompanying high dropout rate of Mexican-American students throughout the Southwest.

In the mountains of northern New Mexico and southern Colorado we talked to people eking out a living on inadequate land. Many of the small villages and towns are depleted in population, their inhabitants having moved on to Pueblo, Denver, Albuquerque, or Los Angeles. Over the past one hundred and twenty years most of these people have lost their lands, and this is the issue that the Alianza de los Pueblos Libres* has dramatized.

Everywhere the grievances were the same: the lack of understanding and the utter neglect shown by local and state government, with the federal government and its various agencies the chief culprits. We heard bitterness expressed toward the police, the welfare agencies, and the school counselor. The entire educational system, including the enlightened universities, stood indicted in the educational crippling of a people. One angry young man said, "We have more enrollees at San Quentin than in all of the colleges of California."

We saw poverty, hunger, despair, and defeat.

But we also saw hope in the eyes of many; we saw the Guadalupe Organization with its grass roots organizing efforts, and solid achievements. The leaders of old established organizations—the Mexican-American Political Association (MAPA), Community Service Organization (CSO), League of United Latin American Citizens (LULAC), American G.I. Forum, and Political Association of Spanish-Speaking Organizations (PASSO)—expressed confidence in their enduring struggle for opportunity, equality, and justice.

We saw the beginnings of the student movement, now grown into a force that must be reckoned with. We witnessed the opening skirmishes of the United Farm Workers Organizing Committee's fight for equal decency for stoop labor. We saw a small, ragged army of grape pickers stand

*Under the leadership of its founder, Reis Lopez Tijerina, the Alianza de los Pueblos Libres has revived the issue of Spanish and Mexican land grants in New Mexico and Colorado. The Alianza is questioning the legality of the means by which the grantees became separated from the land, and seeks to determine whether or not the United States government has violated the Treaty of Guadalupe Hidalgo, which gave assurances concerning language, religion, and land to the people who were conquered during the Mexican-American War.

up to the growers; we watched the groundswell of support for the strikers rise up in the Mexican-American community and spread across the nation. We could discern the beginnings of the Chicano Press Assocation which now numbers some twenty-five independent newspapers. We began to detect a growing unity within the total community: the opening up of channels of communication; the positive indentification with "La Raza"; a commonality of goals and united efforts to achieve them; a surge of leaders whom no one suspected were around; and the emergence of local organizations such as the Crusade for Justice and La Raza Unida.*

At the same time the power structures sensed a threat and a danger. To quell the tide a flurry of activity was initiated. A cabinet-level committee on Mexican-American Affairs was quickly formed. Mexican-Americans began to be appointed to relatively high positions throughout the federal structure. State and municipal governments felt the mood and followed suit; awareness of the change in the wind filtered down to the school systems, the police and welfare departments. Legislators at all levels became concerned. And foundations moved. At this writing the Chicano movement is on its way.

These then are the people to whom we talked over a two-year period. This book is a report and an assessment of what they told us and what we observed. It is to them that we dedicate it.

JULIAN SAMORA

Notre Dame, Indiana
August, 1969

---

*The crusade for Justice, organized by Rudolph (Corky) Gonzales in Denver, Colorado, is a protest group which has been successful in publicizing and helping to resolve various local problems. La Raza Unida organizations are local-action groups originating in the Southwest and presently being formed in Mexican-American communities as far east as Michigan and Ohio.

MEXICAN-AMERICANS
IN THE SOUTHWEST

I

AN OVERVIEW

Considering only the period from 1900 to 1965, the evolution of the Mexican-American ethnic minority in the five southwestern states (California, Arizona, New Mexico, Colorado, and Texas) can be described as one of massive survival of the underlying cultural heritage, accompanied by radical changes in relationships with the surrounding society and in demographic growth.

The cultural survivals have to do with language, manners, behavior values, religion, psychology, and economic status. The great changes have to do with size of population, its distribution, economic activity, and mobility. It has been a period during which striking ups and downs have occurred in the sheer mass of migration from Mexico. Patterns of flow and ebb have been established, disrupted, and reformed in the seasonal migration of hundreds of thousands. Poverty in Mexico has piled up millions of human beings along the border, the concussions and repercussions of which are felt in Oakland, Denver, and Chicago. The villages and towns of the rural hinterland of the United States have been drained of brawn and brains while the urban settlements of the Mexican-American have increased enormously. The resulting clusters have produced clearly discernible areas consistent and peculiar to a degree within themselves and replicating in each the problems common to them all. Within these clusters cores of poverty and retardation of increasing hardness have taken shape; in them the typical syndrome of damaged lives has manifested itself —acute delinquency, social dependence, educational and cultural deprivation, the disintegrating family, and unemployment.

Urban redevelopment has been carried into practice with crushing effects on Mexican communities. Vertical integration, mechanization, and automation have caught up with Mexican hand labor, disrupting or displacing it through radical changes in methods of production and systems of labor marketing. At the same time, a thin line of upwardly mobile professionals and entrepreneurs has appeared and matured and pushed against the resistances of middle-class America, and a small but restless generation of high school and college youth is making itself known. The intellectual issues of acculturation and assimilation have found controversial spokesmen; the long overdue uprising of the national conscience and the fight for Negro civil rights have spread from the black slums to the brown ones; and the war on poverty has been conceived, legislated, reconnoitered, mounted, and dismounted in something less than three fiscal years.

THE ECONOMY

The development of the Southwest has polarized, in stages, around the central movement of enterprise and capital and their attraction of manpower.

By 1900 the railroads had opened the area east and west and had tapped the Mexican borderlands for raw materials and men. The demand for sheer Mexican muscle to lay tracks and maintain rights-of-way lessened gradually until, in the 1950's, it was no longer a predominant factor in the labor market. Thousands of immigrants still made a living in another basic industry, mining; but many times those thousands left the pits and the smelters to seek work in the expanding fields of large-scale commercial farming. These fields were staked out over a very large territory: Michigan, Oregon, central California, the Imperial Valley, Colorado, southern Texas, the midwestern states, and the Great Lakes region. Reclamation advanced, making deserts productive, and technology progressed, making them more profitable and habitable. Cotton became a major crop in California, as in Texas. Packing sheds and canneries drew Mexican workers another step upward and outward. In the two world wars shipbuilding, aircraft construction, and finally electronics drastically changed the economic landscape. Accompanying all this, the building of new tracts, subdivisions, and elite residential zones provided jobs for the increasing numbers of urban Mexican-Americans.

There was a remarkable flux in this vast growth. Manpower needs were filled by industrial recruitment, partly by government agencies, partly by the sensitive grapevine of the workers themselves. These combined to produce the flow and distribution between the slacks and pick-ups of farm labor migration. Domestic employment remained a standby for Mexican women, a small number of whom worked at skilled or semi-skilled jobs in light industry.

On the agricultural side the rough balance between jobs and Mexican job seekers began to receive a series of mounting shocks, hardly perceived by the nation at large. In the 1940's the mechanical cotton picker was introduced in the fields of California. A few years later the recruitment of *braceros* in Mexico began under the sanction of Public

Law 78.* American capital moved south of the border into
the production of cotton, fruits, and vegetables grown for
export to the United States.

On the industrial side, by the early 1950's similar omens
were appearing. Machinery displaced cannery crews, composed in large part of Mexican-Americans. The mechanical
tomato picker was already in commercial use in 1965.

POPULATION DISTRIBUTION

In 1960 the highest figure given for the number of persons of Mexican ancestry (Spanish-speaking, Spanish-surname) in five southwestern states was 3.5 million. Today
it is estimated to be above 5 million, and by 1975 the number will be between 5.5 and 6 million.

The 1960 census distribution by states was as follows:
California 1,453,000; Texas 1,448,000; New Mexico 269,-
000; Arizona 194,000; Colorado 157,000. Thus, in round
numbers, the percentage distribution was 41%, 40%, 8%,
5% and 4% respectively.

There is demographic concentration within each of these
five dominant states. In Arizona the ten largest communities of Mexican-Americans, by counties, totalled 187,000.
(All figures, in round numbers, are from the 1960 U.S. Census.) Maricopa County had 79,000 and Pima County 44,000.
In California, similarly, the ten counties showing the larg-

---

*An executive agreement negotiated between the United States and
Mexico and passed by both Houses of Congress in July 1951, Public Law
78 provided for the recruitment in Mexico of manual laborers—*braceros*—
for employment in agriculture and railroad maintenance in the United
States. Between 1951 and 1960 nearly 3,500,000 *braceros* were transported
to the U.S. for temporary work and returned to Mexico under the terms
of the law. The agreement was terminated in December 1964.

est Mexican-American population had a total of 773,000 persons. The Bay area and metropolitan Los Angeles accounted for 721,000. In Texas the counties of Hidalgo, Bexar, and El Paso, on the same basis of comparison, had 522,000 out of the 912,000 Mexicans living in the state's ten largest communities.

The polarizing effects of migration patterns, jobs, and related factors produced clusters within clusters. In metropolitan Los Angeles, of 576,000 Mexican-Americans living there in 1960, 70,000 were in East Los Angeles; 14,000 in Pico Rivera; 13,000 in Norwalk; 10,000 in Florence Graham; 8,000 in Long Beach; 6,000 in Pomona; and 5,000 in Pasadena. So with the central valley of California. Fresno developed, between 1920 and 1960, into a Mexican-American settlement of 14,000 people surrounded by a fringe of satellite *colonias*—Mendota, Firebaugh, Selma, Huron— with 2,000 to 3,000 each. The San Francisco basin and metropolitan Los Angeles, together, contained 56 percent of all Mexican-Americans living in California in 1960.

The process of impacting continued into the census tracts, which became typically pyramidal in distribution of people. These were the hard cores of county and metropolitan concentration. Of Denver's Spanish-surname population 43,000 were located in 28 census tracts; 56 percent lived in 14 tracts; and six tracts accounted for 12,000 people. Taking the Southwest as a whole, there is a wide range of patterns of residential distribution; but the main trend is unmistakable: concentration within the region, the states, the metropolitan areas and the tracts.

This trend outpaced the percentage growth of the population as a whole. Between 1950 and 1960 the Spanish-surname persons living in California increased by 87 percent, in Arizona by 51 percent, and in Texas by 37 percent. Within each state there was a steady gravitation of people, es-

pecially the young, toward the urban pivots of the region—
Los Angeles, Phoenix, San Antonio, Denver, Fresno. Pueblo and the smaller cities of southern Colorado and northern
New Mexico have functioned as branches, channeling substantial parts of their Mexican populations to Denver County and Albuquerque, which in turn have seen much of this
new growth pass on to Los Angeles. Back of this, of course,
was the migration from a thousand small communities,
falling ever further behind in economic development and
its attendant opportunities.

From the foregoing it would seem that the most helpful
way to take hold of the Mexican-American as a minority
within the Southwest as a region is to consider the areas
that are clearly marked as to geography and percentage of
the population. These are, to repeat: the San Francisco Bay
basin; the central valley of California; the Los Angeles metropolis; the Salt River Valley of Arizona; Denver County;
the upper Rio Grande, loosely embracing southern Colorado and northern New Mexico; south central Texas cen-
tering in San Antonio; and the Border. In broad strokes
these areas may be characterized separately.

The basin of San Francisco Bay includes the following
counties in which large Spanish-surname communities
exist: Alameda (67,000), San Francisco (51,000), San Mateo
(19,000), and Santa Clara (77,000). During the past twenty-
five years foreign trade, merchandising, shipping, light
manufacturing, heavy industry, building construction and
transportation have transformed the uses of land and the
types of livelihood based on them. Agriculture, that once
dominated a green and blossoming expanse around the
bright sophistication of San Francisco, has been reduced to
a green belt drawn tighter notch by notch. Land values as
far south as Gilroy, 75 miles away, have become steadily
inflated. Prune orchards and vegetable farms have given

way to steel mills and electronic complexes. Rapid transit is shaping up as a huge loop of concrete and steel that will enclose the southern half of the basin. When completed it will join central cities and suburbs into a megalopolis of an estimated 7 million inhabitants a few years hence.

Already running out of space, metropolitan San Francisco has begun to reclaim the shallow margins of the Bay itself. On mud banks topped with garbage and debris, instant cities are being projected. Already their forerunners are strung along the western bayshore under fitful canopies of smog. The sounds their dwellers go to sleep by are not those of the surf breaking on Seal Rocks or the lapping of the tide among the marshes. Somewhere within this technological tour de force there will be, in the not distant future, between a quarter of a million and half a million Mexican-Americans. They will have been removed recently from demolished tracts. They will be clinging to the economic fringes of urban existence.

The central valley of California is running a course parallel to that of the Bay area. Ribbons of suburbs reaching from San Francisco to Oakland have already encircled Tracy, Livermore, and Napa, once farming centers and agricultural labor pools. At the northern end of the central valley many Mexican and Negro tracts have been abolished to make way for government buildings and freeways. In the lower half, from Modesto to Tulare, great changes are impending. The San Luis dam, now filling a huge basin at the foot of Pacheco Pass northwest of Fresno, is already throwing its massive weight into the distribution of production, possession, and political power. The signs of this displacement have been showing, here and there, for two decades. They have been perceptible in the removal of the Mexican *colonias* of farm workers from the valley cities, where work was within easy reach, to the shoestring settlements of

shacks and weathered trailers on the western piedmont.
The Mexican-Americans, typically wage earners, are feeling
and seeing only the immediate effects of these deep and
underlying tides of change: new crop patterns, the infiltra-
tion of the rural countryside by small industries, the growing scarcity of rural and urban housing, the mechanization
of food production. The reshuffling will continue—of individuals, of families, of communities. For thousands of
Mexican-Americans, Fresno, Sacramento, and Bakersfield
will increasingly become stepping stones on the way to Oakland or Los Angeles.

It is Los Angeles that stands as the prototype of the
changes that have been taking place during fifty years. The
largest Mexican *barrios* within the county, East Los Angeles
and Boyle Heights, would be sizable cities anywhere. The
smallest, like the one in Torrance, nostalgically still called
the "Pueblo," subsist in the crannies between factories,
mills and refineries. In Pacoima, Azusa, Pico Rivera, and
Norwalk, to name only some, the Mexican-American tracts
continue to lose a small number of rising professionals and
entrepreneurs, and to gain significant increments of poor
people. Within the massive clot of humanity that has covered the county from the crests of Altadena to tidewater
Venice, the *barrios* where Spanish is spoken and Mexican
is lived are locked in the metropolitan sclerosis. Nevertheless, it is here where the widest choice of jobs is found, and
where the common lot sustains, though it be a hard one.
Geographically and psychologically, the county is now the
base for some 700,000 persons of Mexican ancestry. It is
a landlocked base. To the east is the desert. To the south
the spaces between the county and San Diego are filling
rapidly. From San Fernando Valley north a vast and continuous suburb is snaking its way through the Tehachapi
range to Bakersfield, a hundred miles away.

The Salt River Valley of Arizona is the fourth area of interest. Together with Casa Grande and Tucson, the area runs on an axis of about a hundred miles, northwest to southeast. It is one of the major winter tourist centers of the Southwest. At the northern end lies Phoenix, still an important center for the cattle industry, where reclamation has stimulated agricultural progress and provided, around the reservoirs that feed the irrigation canals, the basis for thriving resorts. Phoenix itself contains the largest group of Mexican-Americans in the state. Within the city limits they live in pot-holes of poverty like their contemporaries, the black poor. Outside, small *colonias* wait and watch the steady, encroaching growth. One of these, Guadalupe, a Mexican-Yaqui community of 5,000 people, clings to a barren slope of desert, in the path of a city pushing for a million inhabitants. South of it, and beyond the Valley, the Mexican-Americans of Casa Grande and Tucson ponder the same problems—the cotton-picking machines in the fields and dispossession from *barrios* overtaken by progress.

Much smaller in population, Denver is nevertheless one of the significant pivots in the Mexican-American Southwest. Midway up the eastern slope of the Rocky Mountains between the border and the northernmost Mexican settlements the city of Denver has collected through the last half century the urban drifts of the Spanish-surnamed from the mines, the smelters, the railroads and the farms of Colorado and New Mexico. The tributaries to the growth of the Mexican-American tracts have been cities like Pueblo, Colorado Springs, and Fort Collins. Unlike other cities to which commerce and finance have brought prestige and influence, Denver's blighted core pressing eyeball-to-eyeball against the marts and the countinghouses is comparatively small. Denver can grow comfortably, up and out, for behind it are the soaring playgrounds of international fame and in front of it the spread of the great plains.

Forming a pattern of their own, yet not sharply defined geographically, are the cities and towns and villages of the upper Rio Grande. These are communities such as Alamosa, San Luis, Española, and Las Truchas. Enterprise has bypassed them, and when a sizable investment of the national wealth created the world-renowned center of Los Alamos, its product—atomic destruction—was so exotic that its local economic trickles were modest indeed. In this area massive, overwhelming, unexpected, and radical changes have not happened. The Hispanic-Mexican culture here approaches its Indian ancestry more closely in the life of the family and the small town. It does not disintegrate dramatically. It merely weathers at the edges, losing its lands, its young, and its hopes.

The next area worthy of notice is Bexar County and its urban center, San Antonio. Its real distinction in that part of the Southwest is not so much geographical as it is functional. It is a sort of labor manifold within which the currents of seasonal migration of farm workers sort themselves out. These currents feed in continuous reserves from the lower Rio Grande and feed out streams of men, women, and children who yearly spread to California, Oregon, Colorado, Michigan, and the Middle West. In the winter these migrations retract, and San Antonio becomes their haven. San Antonio has the spongelike quality of poverty and the migrant labor market. It has a high capacity for absorbing those who earn the least and need the most in American society. Like water sopping into a sponge, the Mexican-American poor who commute across the continent to San Antonio disappear into the thousands of cells of the *barrios,* from which they reappear in the spring to the astonishment of outsiders who ask, "But how do they live?"

Finally there is the Border, the one area, if it may be

called such, which exerts a powerful influence on all the rest, an influence which has persisted for fifty years.

It is only by a stretch of the imagination that the Border can be defined as an area, a stretch 1800 miles long between Brownsville and San Diego. No one can safely undertake to interpret the Southwest's Mexican-American who does not reckon with the Border in its multiple and seemingly contradicting roles: the gateway and the barrier; the attraction and repulsion of people on a mass scale; the offer and the denial of economic opportunity; the mosaic of small plans and the chaos of large design between two sovereign states; the legal formalities and the illegal realities; the favorite platform of presidents for speeches on Good Neighborliness and a mighty deployment of military power; a bilingual accommodation of fascinating prospects and a backwash of two cultures; a port of entry and a port of missing men.

Because of its complexity and its durable economic and social effects on people far beyond, south and north, the Border requires a closer look, on both sides.

Mexico's borderlands include six states with a combined international boundary of 2,597 kilometers. In these states are located the following cities with the 1965 census population indicated:

Nogales	39,000
Piedras Negras	45,000
Ensenada	66,000
Nuevo Laredo	93,000
Reinosa	133,000
Matamoros	139,000
Tijuana	166,000
Mexicali	277,000
Ciudad Juarez	309,000

The rate of growth of most of these cities between 1930 and 1950 was extraordinary. Mexicali increased from 6,782 to 171,648 in those two decades. Tijuana had 16,486 inhabitants in 1940 and 148,867 in 1960. Ciudad Juarez, which counted 294,373 residents in 1960, reported only 39,669 thirty years before. Many of these communities and their immediate rural belts attained a rate of growth between 1940 and 1960 in excess of 400 percent, with Tijuana in all probability holding a record of 750 percent.

Population projections for the next fifteen years by Mexican demographers point to continuing, not to say startling, growth in the Mexican borderlands. In 1960 the states of Baja California, Coahuila, Chihuahua, Nuevo Leon, Sonora, and Tamaulipas had 5,734,000 inhabitants. The projections indicate a population of 13,864,000 by 1980. The border cities will no doubt show a corresponding increase.

These are cities of poor people, in the overwhelming mass. They are the terminal points of migratory routes to which the congested cities and the impoverished villages of central Mexico are tributary. The average annual per capita income reported for Tijuana in 1965 was around $1,000 U.S. dollars; for Mexicali, approximately $750. Undoubtedly these figures are on the high side. The average per capita annual income in the same year for border cities has been estimated at slightly under $640. One newspaper statistic hints at the acute overcrowding and poverty that the above figures on population and income suggest. A recent fire that swept three blocks of Tijuana within a quarter mile of city hall destroyed 800 shacks and left nearly 7,000 people without shelter.

That the teeming, congested *barrios* of the Mexican border cities are not truly terminal for the hopes of those who live in them is shown by one striking characteristic of economic life—the border crossings. In 1965 nearly 65,500,000 individual crossings of Mexican citizens under day permits were recorded. They crossed the international boundary to shop and to work. This figure does not include the many thousands of men and women who cross illegally to work on the American side.

The immediate goal of the crossers and line jumpers is the American cities that lie just a step across the boundary —Mexicali, Laredo and Brownsville, among others. A job or a sojourn here is only a breather. These are the ports of entry for hundreds of thousands whose need to keep moving diminishes with the increased distance from the border but is never wholly absent even in the northernmost *colonias*. Hardly an industry in the Southwest that uses raw or semi-trained labor power has not felt the effects of this flux of migration; and few of the social problems of the Mexican-American *barrios* in Los Angeles, Phoenix, Denver and Oakland are not influenced by it.

If to the Mexican migrant the compass of jobs always and unwaveringly points north, it is only because he travels steerage in the economy, the tides of which can change, gradually or suddenly. American capital can flow freely in and out of Mexico. The question whether poor men shall go north or investment shall go south is never finally settled. Now that public opposition holds the *bracero* importation in check, the growing, packaging and processing of fruits and vegetables may move south of the border on a larger scale than in the past. Authoritative voices in the industry have already forecast such a shift on a large scale. No single comment could better illustrate how closely the southwestern Mexican-Americans, such large numbers of whom are only one or two generations removed from migrancy, are webbed with the trends of border life. These trends themselves are reactions to conditions in Mexico, as the poor experience them.

2

MEXICO AND THE SOUTHWEST

The conditions that prevail in the Mexican border states
must be taken into account in any analysis of the Mexican-
American Southwest. More than that. The national policies
of Mexico and the United States—a complicated network
of commercial, financial, strategic, political, and diplomatic
relations—embrace emigration and manpower flow. At any
given time the quid-pro-quo's of national interest on both
sides may produce the opening of the border either to illegal or to managed migration. That is the history of the
period from the 1930's through the 1950's. The shocks to
the southwestern Mexican-Americans that followed were
severe, though they were not registered on the economic
seismographs of an affluent society interested in other mat-
ters. In the broadest possible sense, what happens to the job
patterns, the labor markets, the wage levels, the demographic distribution and even the progress of cultural and political articulation among the Mexican-American minority
is determined by mutually accommodating national policies dictated, on the part of Mexico, by conditions that
make hundreds of thousands of its citizens want to get out.

The most compelling of these is the growth of population, of which the explosion along the border is a measure.

14

Nationally, it has increased from 15 million in 1910 to an estimated 44 million in 1966. In another ten years some Mexican demographers estimate an increase to 61 million people; and by 1980, to 72 million. In the next two decades the Mexican borderlands will continue to operate as they have in the past, serving, as some Mexican observers have already described them, as an "escape hatch" for a society unable to create the 40,000 new jobs every year required merely to hold the line against stark poverty.

The statistics confirm this view. Between 1956 and 1965 nearly 420,000 Mexican citizens were admitted to permanent residence in the United States. The total of admissions in the last fifteen years is over the half-million mark. The seasonal flows within this permanent migration cannot be ignored because they are temporary. In 1965, despite the official demise of the *bracero* program, over 100,000 temporary contract laborers were admitted for seasonal employment. The Border Patrol continues to arrest so-called wetbacks at the rate of more than 40,000 a year. More than 60 million entrants are registered yearly under border crossing permits.

Insofar as this migration stems from the poverty of rural Mexico, it reflects the underlying conditions of land tenure and production. Three and a half million heads of families have received land from the government under the revolution's agrarian reform laws. But, to paraphrase the chorus of "Oklahoma," the Mexican *ejidatarios* and small land workers still don't belong to the land, and the land they are getting isn't grand. The collective farms *(ejidos)* are showing serious weaknesses under the competition of California-style commercial agriculture. The absence of a solid understructure of credit, technical assistance, education, and distribution is gradually reducing the *ejidos*, once hailed as "Mexico's way out," to the status of a losing junior partner of the Mexican economy. On the *ejidos* alone some 11,000,-000 Mexicans depend for their living.

The rewards of agricultural competition are more and more accruing to individual entrepreneurs exempt from acreage limitations and other strictures under the agrarian laws, or encouraged by their lax administration. Still more advantaged are the large commercial operations based on the most fertile land and modern systems of production, irrigation, food processing, and shipping. With wages in harvesting and packing at $2.00 (U.S.) for a nine-hour day there is a surplus of manpower, affording the industry the luxuries of bypassing former *braceros* and the use of police to keep the hiring gates clear.

The more prosperous branches of the new agriculture, moreover, are geared to the export market. Food exports valued at more than 100,000,000 pesos in 1965 included corn, sugar, coffee, shrimp, tomatoes, beef, fresh and canned fruits, and wheat. These and other surplus items—pineapple, honey, strawberries, and cotton, for example—are beyond the buying power of the Mexican wage earner, whose involuntary self-denial supports a large part of Mexico's foreign trade.

The rising volume of consumption of the recent past has most certainly been accounted for by the increase in population and not by a gain in per capita purchasing power. A 1956 benchmark figure has been given by government economists of an average of $40 (U.S.) for monthly earnings in all classes of employment. In spite of a steady upward trend in the gross national product, its distribution in 1966 has not improved in favor of wage earners over the past decade. The effects, in housing alone, are a chronic shortage and standards of shelter of the lowest order.

These and related facts are familiar enough, and are usually treated under the heading of "push factors" behind

Mexican emigration to the United States. Taken together they provide a consistent field of social and economic pressures on the Mexican-American in the Southwest. Up to now, they have been researched and publicized largely with academic emphasis. National policy, on both sides of the border, has taken little notice of such studies. It is not difficult to understand why. The border people most affected by these pressures have not formed a constituency capable of bringing to bear a collective interest on policy. The Mexican-Americans have hardly faced the burden that their peculiar position as a minority in the Southwest has imposed on them. In this regard, as in many others that will be touched upon in this book, they are still searching for their distinctive role in American life.

3

ANALYSIS OF THE
MEXICAN-AMERICAN MINORITY

MOBILITY

No one knows how many Mexicans crossed the border clandestinely between 1910 and 1965—probably as many as 10 million and surely no fewer than 2 million. Since the principal source of information on this point is the reported apprehensions and deportations for illegal entry by the Department of Justice, the estimates undoubtedly reflect gross overlapping and duplication.

The sheer mass of this migration, and the relatively short time in which it was accomplished, were in themselves highly important elements of cultural conditioning. Half a century has been hardly long enough for the Mexican migrants to settle down. As poor people, hundreds of thousands of them were for decades forced into the semi-rootless existence of rural migrancy. To many others the borderlands on the American side were inhospitable. The hope, if not the prospect, of moving north was persistent. The Mexican-American spread to the northwest and northeast has taken place largely since the 1930's, with the establishment of small enclaves in northern cities across the country.

During the past twenty-five years the urban settlements of Mexican-Americans became what the word indicates—settled communities. Continuity of residence in one place

of many of the late migrants characterized the Mexican
neighborhoods. This was mainly due to the self-segregation
of poverty—the gravitation to low-rent neighborhoods. In
these characteristic *barrios* it was possible for the cultural
supports, such as language, to remain vigorous; and it is
within them, too, that the retention of identity made up for
the loss of orientation.

But this stability was precarious. Within the large city
and the metropolis, those who were able to better themselves moved their homes if not their professional or business locations out of the *barrio*. The better paid industrial
workers did likewise. Among the lower income families,
for whom home ownership was beyond reach, shifting residence within the city continued.

This chronic flux within the city was not entirely due to
conditions or attitudes prevailing within the Mexican-
American community. It was also a response to the prevailing conditions and attitudes in the surrounding society:
the abandonment of deteriorating neighborhoods by other
minorities on their way up and out; the dislocations of
World War II; the extensive rebuilding of blighted central
city districts; the hospitality of white Anglo suburbs to
brown Mexican-Americans able to buy a home; the dissec-
tion of the metropolis by grids of freeways. In short, the
Mexican-American in the large cities never quite stratified.
What he lost in cultural compactness, in political harden-
ing, even in defensive angers, he gained in range of social
experience, in wider understanding of the kind of new
society he was in, and in exposure to the tests and temptations of making one's way toward a beckoning American
way of life.

In the rural Southwest the situation was far less subtle.
To begin with, until the mid-fifties a very large group of
Mexicans, the illegals, remained at large, completely cut

off except as exploited men. In California, for example, at
one time there were at least 80,000 wetbacks in temporary
employment. For them a total lack of roots, of family connections, of identity, was essential. The keys to survival
were evasion, transiency and anonymity. Along the border,
from San Diego to Corpus Christi, a twilight zone of unde-
termined depth harbored hundreds of thousands of these
men and women. They were the human currency of cheap
labor, and like money, they were made to circulate.

When the wholesale traffic in illegals declined in the
mid-fifties, its place was taken by another form of equally
mobile manpower, the *bracero*. In fact, one of the virtues
of the *bracero* system from the point of view of its sponsors
was that hundreds of thousands of Mexican citizens could
be imported for a season only, their return home guaranteed by the government. The duration of their employment, however, was long enough to set in motion a
corresponding displacement of settled Mexican landwork-
ers throughout the Southwest. From this time dates the
increasing flow of Spanish-surname people to the large
cities.

It is possible that the simple increase of urban residents
will make for less movement in the future. The principal
reason is that former rural families are less likely to return
to agriculture than they once were to risk the move from
country to town. A few years of living in a large city gives
them an understanding of both ways of life, and one of the
important lessons they learn thereby is that there is, in
truth, no choice of return. A 1965 survey of the Los Angeles-
Long Beach metropolitan area showed that 85 percent of
the Mexican-Americans above the age of five had lived
somewhere in the area in 1960.

A necessary comment on this survey is that migration,
whether urban or rural, is not, contrary to common opin-

ion, a natural tendency of the Mexican-American family. The tenacity with which it holds to the narrowest ledge of opportunity is that of fathers determined to reduce the hardships and hazards of change for their families, of mothers anxious to have continuous schooling for their children, of young men and women wanting to hold on to familiar companions.

THE URBAN TREND

The human traits that make for stability of residence have not, of course, determined the present distribution of the Mexican-American population. Urban growth is a national, not a Mexican-American, phenomenon. The ethnic minorities have only flowed into the channels laid out for them by the twin engineers of change, investment and technology. The Mexican-American city encased by the metropolis, and the Mexican-American slum sedimented within the city, are cultural products of the affluent society, not manifestations of ethnic perversity.

Today more than one-third of the Spanish-speaking population of the Southwest live in the metropolitan compass of 16 cities, including Los Angeles, San Antonio, San Francisco and El Paso. In California the Mexican-American male labor force is over 80 percent urban; in Texas, over 75 percent; in Colorado, New Mexico and Arizona, between 55 and 70 percent. At the rate of growth of the urban percentage of all Mexican-American residents of California between 1950 and 1960 (75.8 percent to 85.4 percent), it could well be that by 1970 more than nine-tenths of them will be living in cities.

Statistics on urban trends do not, of course, probe the significance of what they suggest—that with such massive

shifting and compaction there come correspondingly profound changes in the quality of life. One small example
will serve as an illustration.

In the small rural *colonias* that resulted from the new
waves of migration into the Southwest in the 1920's there
was a credit system at work. It was a variant of the tradi-
tional money lending at usury of rural Mexico. In the
United States it was modified and somewhat mitigated in
the hands of the labor contractor. In the cities this system
has disappeared, and borrowing—since the poor must bor-
row—has presented an entirely new set of subtleties which
baffle the Mexican-American, often handicapped by language. To be sure, there is protection against exorbitant
interest charges and time-payment frauds; but its devices
and services will have to be brought within the understanding and acceptance of the ethnic strangers by education
and institutional outreach.

In the five southwestern states, the forms and conditions
of urban concentration vary. In California, it is obvious
that in another ten years the typically Mexican-American
communities between the massive urban clots will be absorbed. The expansion of suburban construction around
San Diego, Los Angeles, Fresno, and the San Francisco Bay
basin represents a huge enveloping movement around and
through rural California. The old cycle of temporary residence for Mexican-Americans occurred within a circular
chain of rural communities. Increasingly it will be restricted to a few urban bases.

In Texas, unlike California, the open spaces between the
large cities are too vast to fill with creeping suburbia. The
land ownership patterns are too fixed to offer any hope of
dissolving the urban gluts of San Antonio, El Paso, Corpus
Christi and Houston. In Arizona progress will bring more
of the same thing: growth in those sectors least within the

reach of Mexican-American low income workers—electronics and related industries, commercial farming, tourist resorts, and the like.

URBAN REDEVELOPMENT

The increasing number of urban residents has not necessarily produced secure tenancy in the *barrios*. It has, in fact, created the conditions for another epoch of gross displacement. This has come in the wake of urban redevelopment, which has counteracted the half-century drift toward well-defined neighborhoods with a marked ethnic flavor. This displacement is one of the major elements in the current life of the urban Mexican-American who lives in the so-called poverty tracts.

The contrast with the early years of the century is strong. In the period between 1910 and 1920 the comparatively small population of a city like Sacramento or Tucson made it easy for the upper social classes to keep their distance within a small municipal compass. The townhouses and restricted residential neighborhoods—restricted partly by economic status, partly by covenants, partly by unwritten rules of discrimination—left ample space around the industrial parks and the railway yards for crowded low-income neighborhoods. These, the undesirable parts of town, were never too far from the commodious townhouses of the well-to-do.

In the last three decades, because of population increases, values have changed. The "lower part of town" has all along, so it seems, occupied the choicest sites for scenic views and for proximity to river banks, points of speedy exit and entry, and in many cases to historical landmarks. The capitalization of human density has eventually paid off double: in the regular payments of rent through the decades and in inflated value of the ground with the coming of the business and residential high-riser.

It is through these low-income tracts, also, that the modern freeways have found their natural course. Where the high-rent, multiple-story buildings have not already taken over, they follow quickly the routes of the new speedways that pierce the metropolis. At the cloverleafs, junctions, and interchanges huge commercial centers have been built. Culture itself seems to have found a new eminence at the crossroads of the freeway complex. The new monuments to drama, music and the dance were fittingly erected at the vortex of traffic congestions, themselves monumental.

Viewed in retrospect these major shakeups in layout appear more sudden than they actually were. They were in fact preceded by an earlier stage of urban facelifting. It should be recalled that the neighborhoods of weathered, deteriorating or dilapidated housing that developed on the outskirts of many southwestern cities to house Mexican-American laboring families were themselves often buffers between the inner city (the city of insiders might be a better term) and the "hobo jungles" in which a large company of homeless men, and sometimes families, found temporary resting places. These so-called jungles were usually scrubby ditch banks, out-of-the-way groves, expanses of weeds and shrubs flanked by railway tracks and swamps, lonesome water-tank sites and sheltered spots under railway bridges. They were the primitive counterparts of "the lower part of town," where transiency gradually was institutionalized on "skid row." At the end of the harvests these "jungles" were visited by the local police and the undesirables were usually hustled out. Later, when the demand for new industrial sites increased, they were permanently cleared, exposing *colonia* to the next step in urban housecleaning.

Beginning in the 1940's, this development has gained momentum in one southwestern city after another. East Los Angeles has been subdivided into huge blocks bounded by the roadbeds and the overpasses of freeways running north and south, east and west. The Pomona freeway in the process of construction was a gigantic trough four hundred feet across and fifty feet deep in spots where the seediest and densest of the Spanish-speaking *barrios* had once rested on hilltops. In San Antonio the *barrio* around the old Farmer's Market has been demolished, forcing change on hundreds of families. In Tucson industrial depots and night clubs, motels and shopping centers have encircled Pascua Village, long a holdout neighborhood refuge of Yaquis from northwestern Mexico. In San Jose demolition began on a neighborhood heavily populated by Mexican-Americans to make way for a new central city and its attendant freeways; some 1800 families in ten census tracts were eventually affected. In San Francisco some 2700 families and 1900 single individuals, with a large representation of Mexican-Americans, have already been blueprinted out of the Mission District. Through it will pass one part of a huge loop of expressway that will cross the bay, go through Oakland, turn south and meet itself at the southern tip of the bay. There is no statistical certainty possible at this point, but it would not be venturesome to say that in California alone 200,000 Mexican-Americans are in or reasonably close to urban removal. In the metropolis, the *barrio* either disappears or remains as a tiny anthropological relic. Something like this is the fate that attends the small, unincorporated community of Guadalupe, fifteen miles south of Phoenix. At least so its 5,000 Mexican and Yaqui residents fear.

To pose for discussion the intangibles of a major redistribution of the material plant of a society—its public buildings and utilities, its business houses, its monuments, its factories, and the economic plumbing and wiring that join them—is usually unprofitable. The intangibles relate to values or preferences which have little to do with the physical redistribution of assets. There appears to be something eminently proper about urban planning that in one process scatters the blight of the downtown slums and rekindles the sparkle of the central city with high-rising chrome. What makes it germane, nevertheless, to discuss intangibles is that all this is happening in the name of Community; and the successful crash of urban redevelopment through the Mexican-American *barrios* is demolishing such community as the ethnic minority had been able to contrive.

This is a crucial matter. If the city offers anything valuable it is those physical points of intercourse, of exchange, of reciprocity and mutual influence, of services and information, of model and example, of variety in styles. When these points of contact disappear, community has faltered. And that is what has been happening in the Mexican-American low-income *barrios*. These were the taverns, the restaurants, the "joints," the motion picture theaters, the barbershops, the small grocery stores, the dance halls upon which the grapevine of the *colonia* was strung. Usually unprepossessing, often tawdry, never luxurious, they were the best in the way of public life that the neighborhood could afford, and the neighbors were comfortable in them. But their very appearance condemned them to destruction along with the deteriorating housing in which their customers lived. It is necessary to restate the proposition that social communication is far more than a matter of words, which convey both persuasion and meaning most effectively when supported by a thousand overtones of common experience. In this sense, when the lines of communication

of a community are broken, more than telephone wiring
has been torn down. The city planners now moving mas-
sively on the Mexican-American *barrios* have not prepared
a place for the slum dwellers where such communications
can go on in a healthy, secure, economical and pleasant
environment. They must begin all over again.

RURAL LIFE AND WORK

The annexation of the surrounding countryside by expanding cities has absorbed small communities where the
Mexican-American formerly subsisted as a farm laborer.
These were settlements in which a variety of responses to
work opportunities had existed—the day-haul by truck,
the car pool, the family trek to nearby farms at the peak of
local harvests, the seasonal trip to distant places and the
return to home base. What most workers sought, especially
those with families, was residence in an area in which a suc-
cession of seasonal jobs could be pieced together over the
year.

Two kinds of housing were available for those who were
able to achieve this relative stability. One was in the *barrio*
itself where shelter of sorts could be rented, or eventually
bought on time payments. The other, always in shorter
supply, was the on-premises quarters for the farm worker
and his family, often a small barn or converted garage or
remodeled poultry pen.

In agricultural areas lying within 50 to 75 miles of the
rapidly spreading cities, land uses changed. The orchards
and small farms bordering the new superhighways went
first. As they were sold for industrial sites or subdivisions,
the housing for the help was demolished. Jobs and shelter
disappeared together. Thus, for one segment of the Mexi-

can-American rural population, it was not necessary to go to the city to become an urbanite. The city came to the country.

These changes affected logistically the urban labor pool. In the *barrios* that were absorbed by urban expansion, farm-labor contractors set up the familiar pattern of pickups in trucks and refurbished buses. The round trip from home to the fields and back was charged to the worker.

There was a mark of class differentiation between this neighborhood transportation service and the day-haul pickups on "skid row." Here the genuine migrants, the male transients, shaped up in the pre-dawn hours, emerging from and returning to the doss houses that served the row. Mexican-Americans never made up a preponderance of the drifters, at least not until the 1950's. When the *braceros* arrived in large numbers, the Mexican-American contractors lost their pre-eminence as recruiters, and neighborhood transportation service declined.

By the end of the decade 1950-1960 the new outline of work and living was discernible. The massive farm labor pools were in large cities—Oakland, Los Angeles, Phoenix, San Antonio—of which the rural labor pools became satellites with populations in the range of 2,000 to 5,000. The connections between these rural settlements and the urban labor markets became closer, and the differences between them less noticeable. A recent study of unemployed Mexican-Americans in Los Angeles showed that 34 percent of them had come from small rural towns.

To anyone who rode the agricultural circuit of the Southwest in the 1920's the contrast in the latter half of the 1960's is obvious. Citrus groves and orchards have become spotted with electronics plants where improvised packing sheds had once stood. Here a research complex covering several acres has brought in its train hundreds of bedroom tracts to take the place of small farms. There an "instant city" of 60,000 exurbanites has erupted fifty miles from the heart of a metropolis, outflanking the shoestring settlements of rural Mexican-Americans.

As often happens, the stereotypes of former days still cling to the second and third generation of Mexican-Americans. An ethnic minority that was eighty percent rural fifty years ago left an image that is no longer authentic. That image will probably continue to be retouched for decades by the surviving *colonias* that are too unprofitable to be annexed as subdivisions, or too inconvenient to be taken over as industrial sites. But they are already cultural vestiges, waiting for a hometown Malinowski to preserve them in print before they disappear.

OCCUPATIONS

The occupational patterns of the Mexican-American minority follow the trends of migration, urbanization, and technological transformation. That segment of farm labor composed of persons born in the United States is diminishing. It is being replaced by contingents of newcomers whose entry into the labor market is mainly through agricultural employment.

To the cities the former farm hands bring little more than their physical endurance and manual skills. Less than twenty percent, by the last census, of the Mexican-American males in the five southwestern states were employed in other than hand labor occupations. Even on the large commercial farms, where the capability of the Mexican has been abundantly proved in all of the specialized demands of modern agriculture, his progress into the better paid jobs has been slow. However, the Mexican has not been barred

by incompetence or lack of experience from tasks calling for
more than muscle. Where he has been admitted, there has
been no lowering of performance standards. What *has* been
lowered is wage scales. In the booming 1960's, irrigators
and tractor drivers in some districts work for a dollar an
hour, and might be willing to work for less if *braceros* and
illegals were available.

The main occupational opportunities for the urban
Mexican-Americans have been in the construction industry,
the clothing trades, domestic services, building maintenance, restaurants and hotels, gardening and landscaping,
trucking and retail selling.

A series of analyses by the U.S. Department of Labor's
Bureau of Labor Statistics published in the Plans for Progress report of August, 1964–December, 1965 provide data
on the occupational distribution of the Spanish-speaking,
excluding farm labor. Employment in 291 companies filing
Plans for Progress reports in 1965 showed only 108,759 persons of Spanish surname out of 7,091,040 employees. Of the
Spanish-surnamed employees only 2.4 percent were officials
and managers; 2.6 percent professionals; 2.4 percent technicians; 3.3 percent sales; 13.1 percent office and clerical.
Of the 76.2 percent blue collar workers, 40.8 percent were
production workers; 15.6 percent craftsmen; 15.4 percent
laborers and 4.4 percent service workers.

As the Mexican-American penetrates the upper brackets
of skill and wages his numbers thin noticeably. The escala-
tion is slow and does not carry with it the mass of the Spanish-speaking minority.

ECONOMIC STATUS

Poverty and minority are synonymous for a large segment
of the Mexican-American population. According to the

1960 census there were 243,000 families in the Southwest who were living in poverty commonly described as stark. In these families there were 1,100,000 individuals, of whom 530,000 were minors under 18 years of age.

The Mexican-American registers a far greater percentage of the poor than of the total population. Of the 11,312 poor families in Arizona (1960) more than 30 percent were Spanish-surnamed. In California, where one out of ten residents was of Mexican ancestry, two out of ten of all poor families belonged to this ethnic group. Over half of the impoverished families in Texas were Mexican. The starting rung of the economic ladder for these families in south Texas was a median income of $2200 a year.

Such a level of income per family was on a par with the per capita figures for the border counties. For Starr County it was $534; for Laredo, $937. In one Denver County tract, where poverty is compacted and compounded, 73 percent of the families had incomes of less than $4,000 and 27 percent had incomes below $3,000. California, still the golden west to the Mexican-American of Texas and Colorado, has done no better by him. About 20 percent of all families had an income of $3,000 or less in 1960. It was probably lower in 1965, when a special census showed that in some sections of metropolitan Los Angeles incomes had fallen from the 1960 levels. The exploitation of low-wage labor from Mexico is no longer the well-kept secret it once was. In 1964 most wage earners who performed agricultural work in that year obtained an average of under 150 days of employment and earned an average of $935.

For the Mexican-American, income and geographical latitude are related. An income of $3,000 for a Mexican family living in Calexico is already 500 percent higher than the median across the border in Mexicali. And the $6,000 median in the San Francisco Bay area is twice that of Calexico. Abacus economics would seem, therefore, to produce the optimistic calculation that the farther north the Mexican-American goes, the higher he rises.

It is necessary to place the tables, graphs, and data of census reports against the entire panorama of ethnic minority life in the Southwest. The point of the comparison is unmistakable: the Mexican-Americans are the region's most excluded from the possession and enjoyment of its wealth.

UNEMPLOYMENT

The most obvious aspect of the minority economic status is the lack of work. Random data from census tracts throughout the Southwest show rates of unemployment of 7 percent to 10 percent of the male labor force. Thus many localities which are rated normal in unemployment rates as they apply to the total labor force would be placed in the crisis category with respect to the Mexican-Americans.

To track down the percentages until they lead to the worst pools of unemployment is to show a lack of respect for the dignity of averages. Yet this is not to exaggerate but simply to suggest how low the bottom of the totem pole really is for some.

In Los Angeles unemployment rates of 12 to 25 percent have been found in some Mexican-American neighborhoods. One Denver County tract showed a rate of 20 percent. At the low point of production in agriculture in the Lower Rio Grande, the Salt River Valley, the Imperial Valley, and the vast central valley of California, there are communities where a third of the available manpower is idle.

There are peculiar elements to be taken into account in

assessing the ultimate meaning of such figures. One is that unemployment reporting is significant only as it applies to workers covered by unemployment insurance. In *colonias* where farm employment is more than marginal no statistics will accurately reveal the true state of affairs.

The historical role of the Mexican has been to keep the supply of manual labor well ahead of demand. This role has not changed substantially. Economic opportunity for him has always been governed by the two variables of input of men into the labor market and technological change.

ECONOMIC OPPORTUNITY

The input factor is the simplest to describe. It is but a different name for the history of immigration since 1910. Almost the whole of that history can be considered in terms of the open border, the traffic in wetbacks, and the period of the *bracero*. These were, each in turn, responses to the demand for raw manpower while the Southwest was busy clearing and leveling the land, reclaiming its deserts, staking its claims, and connecting everything with tracks and roads. This is why, when John Nance Garner made his eloquent plea for unrestricted immigration in the 1920's, he was speaking for all who appreciated the importance of Mexican brawn.

Between 1910 and 1940 the earliest immigrants settled down and their number made an important difference. Theirs became the vested interest of the established *locales* for whom the continuing flow of new migrants became the ebb of their own chances for economic betterment.

Economic opportunity for the low-skilled Mexican-American in the last twenty-five years has been affected by two factors: the continuing inflow of jobseekers like himself; and, simultaneously, by the upgrading of skills in the new areas opened by an increasingly sophisticated economy.

Technology has also upset many of the old standbys of employment. Mechanization in canneries and other food processing plants has eliminated thousands of jobs. This was a significant turn, for cannery work had been for forty years the next leg up and out of farm labor. In the cities, mechanization has shown a tendency to catch up with and outrun those who have turned there for a livelihood. Laundering and car washing are examples.

This condition is now familiar to Mexican-Americans in every part of the economy. Commercial agriculture has at last perfected the mechanical tomato picker, with about as drastic an effect on jobs as the cotton-picking machine produced fifteen years before.

In the low-wage occupations transiency has been a characteristic handicap of the Mexican-Americans as a group. The footholds of residence and well-paid work have been only for the few among the immigrants of the last four decades.

SMALL BUSINESS

It is from these lucratively employed few that a small merchant sector has emerged—small both in numbers and in economic importance. Typically the *barrio* entrepreneur is a restaurant keeper, a grocer, the publisher of a newspaper with limited circulation, a building contractor, self-employed mechanic or craftsman. Bakeries and *tortillerias* provide opportunities for investment on a small scale and are characteristic of the business side of the ethnic neighborhood. Supplying materials and equipment for these consumer services are a few larger processors and manufacturers located in the principal cities of the region.

The small businessman who has made the *colonia* his base has never monopolized its limited market. On the one hand, Mexican entrepreneurs who discovered during the turbulent years of the revolution that their capital could find uses north of the border restricted their business to the large and growing Mexican population there. On the other hand, non-Mexican merchants have always found it profitable to operate in the *barrio* their "five-and-tens," their army surplus outlets, and their supermarkets for the Spanish-speaking clientele.

The Mexican-American entrepreneurs have become numerous enough to create their own chambers of commerce and luncheon clubs among the younger business set. As a class they have not yet proved to be effective accumulators of capital. Behind them there have been no powerful sources of credit to float them into the "big time" of commerce or manufacturing. Some have made sizable fortunes in real estate speculation, medicine, and publishing. But they have yet to prove themselves the aggressive and successful builders of chain stores, entertainment syndicates, drug networks, or insurance companies. In all of these areas of risk and profit there are individuals who are testing their nerve and putting up their cash, adumbrating perhaps the rise of a brown bourgeoisie. It will take another generation at least to show that the Mexican-American is capable of being thoroughly acculturated in this respect also.

For the present this component of a modest middle class keeps close to the protective coloration, the sentimental attachments, the cultural identifications, the mix of language, and other ambivalences which make a spectrum rather than a bloc of the Mexican-American ethnic minority. This role the small businessmen share with the professionals.

HOUSING

The kinds of houses Mexican-Americans live in are the most visible index of their place in the present society of the Southwest. There is a certain range of dilapidation. There are within the most rundown *barrios* brightly painted cottages with fenced-in flower gardens that set themselves off by a defiant trimness. But such possessions are not the norm. Home ownership can run as low as 15 percent in some communities, as high as 50 percent in others. In either event, landlords have not had the will or tenants the resources to attack a housing blight which is among the worst in America.

Originally, these settlements were the railroad and farm labor pools of the early century. Ground space was ample. One may still see the wide, unpaved streets laid out in the once open landscape that was unattractive to all but squatters and sagebrush brokers. As remarkable was the free space above, for those were the days before the residential tower. Even in their weatherbeaten and grim obsolescence Mexican-American neighborhoods that have not yet been visited by the bulldozer offer lessons in living. The men and women who put shacks together from secondhand and discarded materials did not build in the spirit of a vendetta against plant life. The economic scale in these reservations of poverty was small indeed, and perhaps for that reason, inevitably it was a human scale.

These were the sunshine slums pioneered by the Mexican and later adapted by the Negro. They still house hundreds of thousands of Mexican-American poor. Today 35 percent of the occupied dwellings in East Los Angeles are classified as unsound, dilapidated, and in varying stages of disrepair. These are mostly rented dwellings. In a hard core poverty tract of Houston 90 percent of the residential structures were built in 1939 or earlier. When the residents of Guadalupe, Arizona recently took stock, they found that out of 677 dwellings 500 were substandard homes with outside toilets. In Phoenix the new skyscrapers look down on decaying dwellings surrounded by affluence.

There has always been some residential dispersion from poverty tracts, and this may become more common as additional central city *barrios* are demolished. Normal dispersion has taken place when family income increased and living standards rose. Contemporary displacement by sudden sweeps of rebuilding is of a different order. It is involuntary. Its possible long-term advantages for the integration and acculturation of the few must be weighed against the short-term anxieties of the many who must move.

EDUCATIONAL OPPORTUNITY

The course of immigration, demographic distribution, transiency, occupational mobility, neighborhood status, and income have all in some way affected the chances of the Mexican-American child to keep up with the national norms of educational attainment. In some communities immediately north of the border, between 70 and 90 percent of the residents are Spanish-speaking. Persistent failure to consider bilingualism a cultural asset has made it an additional problem rather than a promising opportunity. What might have been a cultural bonus still remains, in many parts of the Southwest, a handicap for the young whose home language is Spanish.

The self-segregation of poverty left its mark on the schools. It has not been overcome by residential mixing. A recent survey of the public schools of San Jose, California showed a marked dominance of Mexican-American stu-

dents in some districts. Of six schools serving mixed neighborhoods but located in or close to *barrios* the school with
the best ethnic balance had a 53 percent majority of Mexican children and the school with the greatest imbalance
had a majority of 87 percent.

One need not lodge a special grievance against the public schools that have served the Spanish-surname communities to assess the high dropout rates and other causes of
educational retardation. The gap between the Mexican-
American minority and the rest of the population is ample
evidence of failure to provide equal educational opportunity.

The median number of school years attained by Mexican-
Americans fourteen years old and over is as follows: Arizona
8.3; California 9.2; Colorado 8.7; New Mexico 8.8; and
Texas 6.7. These are averages. They conceal drastic imbal-
ances in areas of near-total social deterioration. In a Houston tract it was found that the average was 5.4 years, against
which an average of 5.7 in some border counties seemed a
hopeful improvement. In Denver it is quite probable that
Mexican-Americans, with an average of 8.6 years of instruc-
tion in some localities, are four full years behind the general
population. Riverside, California is some fifty miles from
Los Angeles, which has been called the Ultimate City. If
the cultural opportunities which such a title presupposes
have reached Riverside, the census data do not show it.
The Spanish-surnamed living there report an average of
6.7 years of schooling.

Such figures, to be sure, conceal the weight of all the
factors noted earlier. It is extremely unlikely, for example,
that the half million emigrants who have been absorbed
by the Southwest since 1950 were among Mexico's best edu-
cated citizens. Their lack of opportunity was the fault of
their native, not their adopted country. Nevertheless, the

effects must be set down out of statistical necessity in the United States census reports. With all due allowances, it is necessary to say that society and the schools are still capable of producing situations such as this one: The town of Guadalupe in Arizona has over 5,000 inhabitants, all Mexican-American. It is a stable, slowly evolving community, not given to sudden growth. Between 1910 and 1965 only 38 of its youth were graduated from high school. None had completed college.

An educational attainment of eight years or less is automatically bracketed with the occupational capability and income level of a manual worker. As automation invades clerical and related occupations, educational preparation for those who are to hold the new jobs must advance at least through high school and, sooner or later, beyond. As an ethnic group, therefore, the Mexican-Americans have a present handicap of from four to seven years vis-a-vis the rest of the population. The rapid general increase in high school and college enrollment of the recent past serves but to emphasize the gap. The observation that the Mexican-American must run hard just to keep from falling back even more, is hardly an exaggeration.

Public Assistance

The race is not only to qualify for jobs but also to avoid dependence on public assistance. The welfare load of Spanish-surnamed recipients far outruns their percentage of the population. The figures are familiar enough. The regional averages do not vary greatly from those recently given for Denver: 46 percent of those receiving aid to dependent children and 67 percent of those receiving general assistance have Spanish surnames. In Texas, 40 percent of the recipients of aid to dependent children are families with Spanish surnames, while in California 22.8 percent of those receiving similar benefits are Mexican-Americans.

A more impressive way to view the situation is to visit the waiting rooms of the public welfare agencies in any southwestern city, or to do the rounds with social workers on caseload tours. The house calls are in the tracts where unemployment runs from 8 to 20 percent, where the deterioration of residences is 40 percent or worse, where median years of schooling do not go above the elementary grades, and where the reported income per family ranges from $2,500 to $3,000. The call-up of the needy over the loudspeakers as they wait their turn in anterooms sounds like the rollcall of a *barrio*. In these public places it is the women and the children who put the best face possible on poverty. In five out of ten cases it is probably a brown face.

But the southwest society of Mexican-Americans must be regarded from still other points of view. In a sense the terms Mexican-Americans, Spanish-speaking, Spanish-surnamed are convenient sociological handles and statistical catch terms. The use of these terms and of others—Mexicans and Spanish-Americans—suggests at once the history of the region, its population movements, and its mixtures of culture. The future might well force this ethnic minority to close ranks against hostility or pressure in the name of racial identity; it might also loosen internal ties by more intense acculturation and assimilation.

Trade Unionism

The relationship of the Mexican-American to the trade unions has been ambivalent. On the fringes of the labor market, where the Spanish-speaking jobseeker makes his first connection, he has been hard to reach and even harder to organize. From this substantial reservoir come the moonlighters, the recruits for the open shop, the victims of unethical employment agencies, and the illegals. Adult workers who have been in the United States only a short time are total strangers to the requirements and the ideology of American trade unionism. When faced with the closed shop, the payment of dues for the union card is often regarded as the purchase price of a job.

In many industries of the Southwest, organizing campaigns and plant elections must now reckon with a Spanish-speaking constituency. Considering that this reservoir of labor power is one from which widely divergent industries draw, the unionizing problems created are common to all unions. They have, however, chosen to concern themselves only at the critical times of a campaign or an election, and purely from the point of view of the particular union affected. Trade-unionism as a national or regional organization has never, in the Southwest, approached Mexican-Americans as a cultural and social entity within which the ideas and attitudes of economic democracy could be planted.

Eventually there has developed within many unions a significant Spanish-speaking membership which by dint of experience has learned the way of collective economic action and accepts its discipline. From these ranks have emerged Mexican-American trade-union leaders, mainly in the shop steward, plant representative, and business agent categories. The higher they have risen, however, the closer they have come to the frustrations and temptations of power controls and politics within the unions. Informal blocs along ethnic lines have tended to emerge, rarely for the purpose of sharpening some ideological issue or moving the understanding and militancy of the rank and file to the next higher level. With hundreds of thousands of Spanish-speaking men and women in the ranks of organized labor there has never been an effort to mobilize them in an auxiliary but distinctive affiliation, as has happened among Negro trade-unionists.

In short, some fundamental questions are still to be raised in this important area of the life of a great many working Mexican-Americans in the Southwest. They are now too numerous in and out of trade-unionism to be thought of casually. In some industrial plants in Texas and California one half or more of the membership is Spanish-speaking. One of the largest locals of a construction union, with 15,000 members, has a registered membership that is 60 percent Mexican. A garment workers' union with 8,000 members is 75 percent Spanish-speaking. Since these are industries on which unemployment presses severely, trade-unionism is face to face with the Mexican-American and must deal with him in and out of the union hall.

THE PROFESSIONS

The dismal averages of educational attainment already cited and the slow economic and professional advance reflected by percentage formulas tend to obscure the qualitative importance of such advance. The effect on the Mexican-American community of the professional man or woman in its midst is a pervasive, though subtle one. Ethnic pride is invigorated whenever an individual of a minority becomes an attorney, a doctor, a professor, or a civil servant. There is more confidence in the approach to the bureaucracy and the due process of the general society through an intermediary speaking one's own language and having a familiar cast. Often the confidence is misplaced but its human roots persist. Moreover, the first generation of the successful ones is very likely carrying vivid personal memories of deprivation, of rebuffs, personal confrontations with ignorance or prejudice, as well as of sympathy received or understanding offered in time of need.

These elements are present in the new generation of Mexican-American professionals. In proportion to the ethnic group as a whole, the professionals are few indeed. Their distribution by professions can be surmised from the figures compiled from the 1960 census for California. There were 21,405 Spanish-surname persons engaged in professional, technical and related work, of whom 3,599 were teachers, and 2,645 were state civil servants. This represents a very small percentage of both the total professional population and the Mexican-American minority—ratios profoundly affecting the character of the continuing relationships between this select group and those who remain far behind in economic and cultural opportunity.

From all that can be observed, most of those who are upward bound carry few burdens of ethnic commitment. A smaller number do carry such commitments, sometimes at personal risk and often at personal cost, not having yet found the way to make their influence more effective through combined action. It is from their thin ranks, moreover, that public agencies recruit for appointments to more attractive staff positions. Within the Mexican-American community there are no comparable opportunities. The decisions that are made by individuals tell a great deal about the process of assimilation by the general society, with its distribution of values between personal advancement and collective progress.

A process of self-selection is at work among Mexican-Americans who have risen high enough to catch the ear and the eye of those who are in a position to distribute the resources, appointments, honors, and opportunities of acceptance by the general society. Some, in their professional careers, must define the terms of these transactions and determine whether they are to render genuine or merely nominal representation of millions of Mexican-Americans on important issues. A few have already chosen the way of service to their people. The task is to identify them and bring them together.

THE INTELLECTUALS

The question of leadership of the Mexican-American minority is being raised seriously, and for the first time from an intellectual point of view, by a still smaller kernel of teachers and college professors who have maintained an active interest in and connection with their communities. Most of these individuals are not themselves contenders for leadership. Bound by emotional ties to their ethnic origins, they are equipped with the intellectual discipline to examine leadership roles more critically, whether these roles are assumed by friendly outsiders or by ambitious insiders.

This scrutiny of community leadership is integral to the consideration and ultimate resolution of other issues: the creative uses of bilingualism; effective political participation; Negro and Mexican-American relations; the role of research in ethnic progress; the rewards and hazards of cultural accommodation; current theories of community organization as applied to the Mexican-American *colonias;* Mexican policy, American diplomacy, and the effects of both on life in the Southwest; the significance of labor organization to ethnic minorities; the adaptation of educational systems to youth and adults.

Dialogues on subjects such as these, while not entirely

novel, are involving more minds. Fittingly enough, it is the colleges and the universities that have stimulated this advance; but as yet they have made no effort to relate it to a wider field of intellectual exchange and perhaps give it a more effective platform.

To make such an effort is important. Young men and women are now tentatively exploring the separate facets of the central issue of progress within the American society —acculturation, assimilation, integration. Using rational tools they have begun to master—research, publication, criticism—they are engaged in self-examination and social appraisal. Though they may not be entirely aware of it, their conversations shuttle between subjective anxieties and the social problems of the minority they are rapidly leaving behind. Should the frail dimension of ethnic awareness be suffocated or wither from neglect, it would unquestionably be a loss to the general society as well as to the minority.

The Students

In 1964 nearly 750 Spanish-surnamed students were enrolled at Los Angeles State College. They are to be found today in every major university and in many smaller institutions of higher learning. The number graduated from California colleges in 1964, according to one estimate, was over 2,500.

Although the absolute numbers may be encouraging, taken by themselves they are misleading. Accepting the 2,500 figure as true, it would still be less than one percent of all the graduates of that year. The Spanish-surnamed residents of California comprise more than ten percent of the total population.

In a 1965 survey involving 10,000 students in five south-ern California universities, only 75 were students with Span-ish surnames. The Berkeley branch of the University of California recently listed 77 Mexican-Americans among its 25,000 students. The University of California at Los Ange-les had 70 Mexican-American students in a campus enroll-ment of 26,000.

This imbalance marks one course of action for the future —a very large increase in educational opportunities for more young people to complete college careers. The other is the stimulation and guidance of those who are already on campus and are, in their own way, pondering the prob-lems of the ethnic minority from which they have sprung. One of these problems is the stimulation of high school students to set their ambitions on a college education. An-other is the ways and means of serving the *barrios* in their concerns. There is incipient organization among the stu-dents of various campuses to these ends.

THE YOUNG

Significant as they may be in numbers, the Mexican-American university and college students are only a tiny elite as compared with the young people of high school and elementary school age. There are approximately 1,750-000 primary, intermediate, and secondary school students of Mexican descent in the five southwestern states. In the largest Mexican community, that of East Los Angeles, a 1965 survey established that 37 percent of its population were children fourteen years of age or younger. This exam-ple is typical of other communities. Young people account for a large part of the Mexican-American minority.

Among the very young, different, though equally pressing, cultural gaps appear. On one side stand the impoverished households, the alien family style, the ancestral language, the insecure community. On the other there is the school with its inadequate budgets, its administrative molds, its distance from the families of its pupils. Between them is the preschooler who speaks only Spanish, who falters in his first and crucial encounter with Anglo American because his native speech is still regarded as a barrier and not a road and because in addition he brings with him all the handicaps of poverty.

Unfortunately, it is apparently not yet fully understood at all levels of government that very large investments of money and effort are needed to compensate for the years of neglect. The cutting of federal aid to education, and particularly the failure to appropriate more than a fraction of the funds authorized by Congress for the federal bilingual education program* has resulted in the cancellation or rejection of many experimental projects aimed at helping the Spanish-speaking child who is just beginning school.

SELF-HELP

Some of the most obvious and satisfying efforts at self-help in the *barrios* have been in the establishment and maintenance of cooperative child care centers, where Mexican-American teachers and mothers serve on a voluntary basis. There are other manifestations of this spirit.

It is probably a sociological truth that the greater the distance between the Mexican-American culture of the

---

*Title VII of the Elementary and Secondary Education Act (ESEA). Congress authorized $30 million for this program for fiscal 1969 but funds were not appropriated until late 1968, and then the appropriation was only $7.5 million.

colonia and the help-yourself incentives of individual advancement, the more numerous the acts of mutual aid and support. Before they became familiar with institutionalized social work, the Mexican migrants were imbued with the simple idea of neighborliness as a relief of urgent family need. The constant exchange of small quantities of food— a cup of lard, two ears of corn, a few coffee grains—that took place in a Mexican village did not totally disappear after emigration. When emigrant families found it possible to buy onions or beans or rice in one-hundred-pound bags, thereby saving measurably in their food outlays, they began the practice of cooperative buying, partly to share the savings, partly to avoid spoilage because of lack of refrigeration.

These were some of the precepts of poverty, not necessarily the manifestations of nobility or altruism. They still prompt individuals to respond to needs that reflect new stresses or demands—interpretation in court and other public and private institutions, the never-ending repair of very used automobiles, the sharing of a telephone, the endless counseling of individuals through a daily round of perplexities. Not infrequently several families have, by taking turns, joined in moving condemned bungalows or cottages to a distant *barrio,* thus distributing the heavy labor that no one man could provide.

The important thing to notice in these services of mutual help is their scale. This has always been immediate, concrete, to the root of the matter, not susceptible to administration by third parties, and always creating and reinforcing a sense of obligation for some future time. There are persons living in the *barrios* who still remember these customs, and who still follow them. They are a significant element in the pattern of community life evolved by the Mexican-American over the decades.

COMMUNITY ORGANIZATIONS

Following the end of World War II most of the Mexican-American organizations focused their interest on neighborhood improvement, protest against police harassment and brutality, election reforms, citizenship and naturalization, and funeral insurance protection. Underlying these interests, two factors have conditioned the present forms of cooperative action, now generically called community organization, among Mexican-Americans. One of these elements is the abiding preference for self-help. The other is the as yet unbridged gap between social service institutions, welfare agencies, and similar bodies and their clients. The latter condition, in its most recent and probably least durable manifestation under the Office of Economic Opportunity, is discussed in chapter 5.

Among the spontaneous forms of mutual aid there have been the funeral societies, the *mutualistas,* and similar organizations. But these have been only one segment, and not the most enterprising or outreaching, in the ferment of organization that has occurred in the last twenty years. One group has claimed that it was in active contact with no less than three hundred Mexican-American organizations in the Los Angeles metropolitan area. The figure is not improbable, though it does not give any clue as to the degree of organizational activity present. The mortality rate is known to be high.

If the effectiveness of organizing activity has been checked by frequent failures and discouraging frustrations, there has nevertheless been laid a foundation of accomplishments and experience. Many groups can now reckon their survival by the years instead of by the months. In the fifteen years between 1950 and 1965 the various organizations achieved a voter registration of over 400,000 Mexican-Americans in

California alone. They have won recognition through local efforts for civic improvement with respect to policing, health services, street lighting, and garbage disposal.

Self-starting community action has not confined itself to the irritations of urban housekeeping. From within the Mexican community have come voices and organized protest against job discrimination, exclusion from public services, and segregation in schools. The earliest victories in the courts against the "separate but equal" doctrine were won in the mid-forties. The court's words in the *Mendez* vs. *Westminster* case* could have been the curtain raiser to the civil rights movement ten years later: "Such methods are not conducive . . . to the inculcation and enjoyment of civil rights which are of primary importance in the public school system of education in the United States."

No less significant or historic on a national scale, was the prolonged and finally successful campaign against the *bracero* system of labor. Over a twelve-year period this campaign, launched in the Mexican *barrios* of California and sustained practically without funds through a series of economic actions, legislative presentations, publicity, and research, reached wider circles of a national audience, until in the final three years, it was concluded with the repeal of Public Law 78. By that time it had become a drawn battle between commercial agriculture and a coalition of labor, religious organizations, and their sympathizers.

Several clichés about the Mexican-Americans have collapsed in the unfolding of these events. One was that they

---

**Mendez et al.* v. *Westminster School District of Orange County.* A complaint brought by Mexican-American parents alleging "an invasion by common school authorities of the equal opportunity of pupils of Mexican ancestry or descent as a result of their segregation, to acquire knowledge . . ." Federal Court, southern district, California central division. February 18, 1946. The text of the decision appears in 64 Federal Supplement, p. 544.

Pre-Columbian statue, Hemisfair — San Antonio

Foreground: El Paso; background: Juarez, Mexico

Strikebreakers catch farm labor bus at border — Roma, Texas

Commuters await international streetcar — El Paso

Aluiso, California

Mendota, California

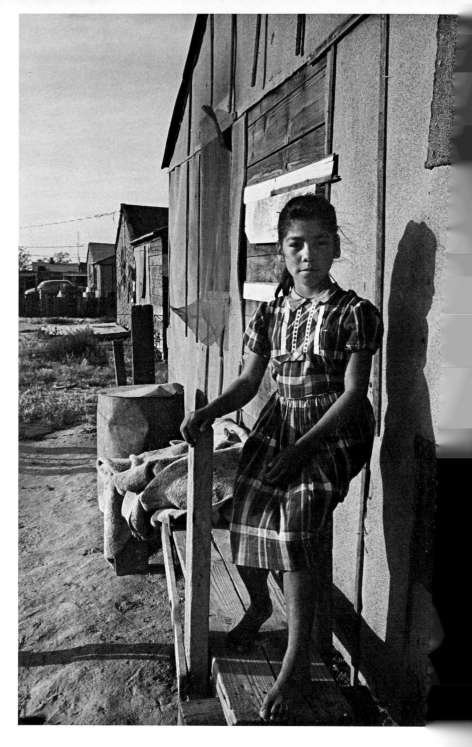

Three Rocks, California

Denver

Porterville, California

Rancho de Taos, New Mexico

Los Angeles

Guadalupe, Arizona

El Paso

University of Texas — El Paso   *Photo courtesy Los Machos of Laredo*

Los Angeles

Guadalupe, Arizona

Delano

Los Angeles

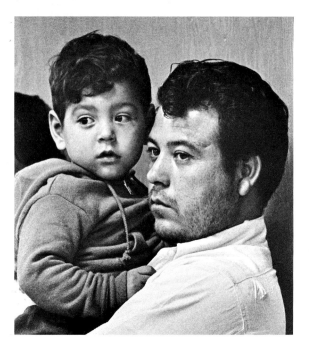

Visalia, California

Tenants' meeting — El Paso

Calexico, California

Los Angeles

Los Angeles

Del Rey, California

Delano

National Farm Workers Association rally — Fresno

San Antonio

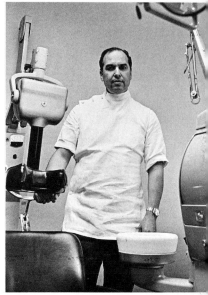

Dentist — Los Angeles

Teacher — Lindsay, California

Editor — Los Angeles

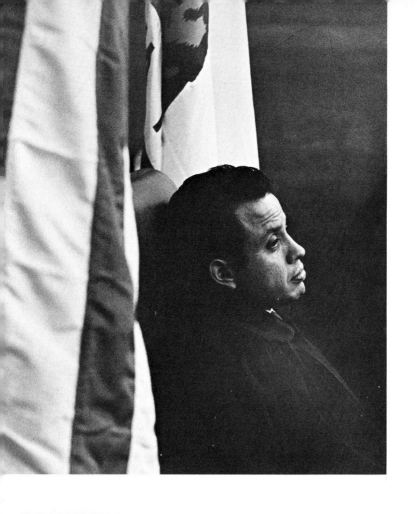

Automated molybdenum mill — Red River, New Mexico

Cabinet manufacturer
— Denver

Trade instructor
— Los Angeles

University professor — Tempe, Arizona

High school chemistry lab — San Antonio

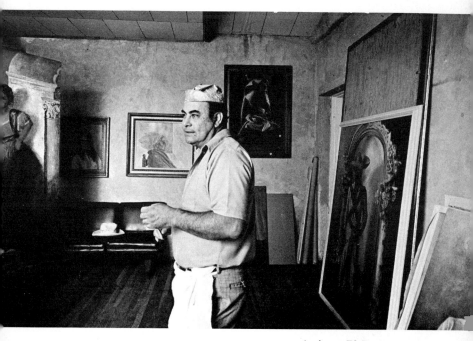

Artist — El Paso

have no will to resist economic mistreatment or social discrimination. Another was that they have no capacity to organize. Still another, that there is a dearth of leadership ability among them.

These are stereotypes, and they persist for a number of reasons. There is no history of these events written and circulated so that it comes to the attention of more than a small circle of specialists. In the waste and futility of *barrio* politics the lessons of organizational failure have been neglected. The leadership cadre has been small and overtaxed. Practical experience in democratic group procedures that expedite results and minimize pointless talk has been limited to the few. Funding has been scarce. Methods of obtaining community cooperation have been too uncritically borrowed from the larger society, with a resulting strain that many groups have not been able to survive. Intensely human endeavors have been pitched on a scale too large for *barrio* citizens to grasp, plan, direct, and administer themselves.

To point to these difficulties is not to minimize the significance of community cooperation sustained by Mexican-Americans during the past three decades, It, too, is a new dimension in the life of this minority, the one which perhaps most pointedly indicates promising change.

NATIONAL ORGANIZATIONS

After World War II much of the organizing vitality among the Southwest's largest minority was provided by the young war veterans. They formed organizations of their own, notably the American G.I. Forum, or joined with a newfound pride other groups which were seeking more effective and satisfying roles for Mexican-Americans.

Passing by stages through state organizations predominantly of a political orientation, Mexican-Americans have begun to sort themselves into leagues and forums with regional and national aspirations. Their organizers and driving spirits are members of the professions and small businessmen who have reached the limits of status locally. The frankly political organizations raise issues dealing with appointment to public posts of Mexican-Americans, participation in the electoral processes, broadening of professional opportunity, and election of Mexican-Americans to legislative bodies. The non-political groups target discriminatory practices, deficient educational services, civil liberties, rundown housing, and other conditions which particularly affect the *barrios*. Because of their articulateness, and because they are the only visible entities with real or assumed political weight, they are the channels through which high-level contacts with the minority are made by the institutional powers.

Like all of the volunteer organizations to be found in Spanish-speaking communities, these organizations carry on because of the intense activity of a few. The financial demands of organizing activity are met by constant improvisation, the dues-paying base being too limited for the scope of the undertakings. Undoubtedly it is in the ranks of organization activists that men and women who are ready and willing to play more ample roles in community affairs are found. Such talent, indeed, is the most easily co-opted for service in official bureaucracies, which is at once a measure of success and a loss to the organization.

Aware that as yet their individual assets do not accord any one of them predominance in the affairs of the minority community, the groups are constantly in search of unity. This has been up to now a precarious balance of personalities rather than a compromise of forces or ideological positions. In the attendant maneuvers the leaders show a refined mastery of tactics, parliamentary and other. Unity has found expression in episodes that are both dramatic and symptomatic. Through their widespread support for the Delano and Rio Grande Valley strikes Mexican-Americans united in protest against the denials of social legislation and collective bargaining long suffered by farm workers. In the now familiar "Albuquerque walkout" they were unanimous in declaring that this ethnic minority has come of age.

With all their handicaps, these regional and national organizations are the only existing means of stimulating some semblance of ethnic consensus. They occupy an upper level for the transmission and publicizing of collective thinking on current issues. This level, however, is still insulated by vacuums above and below. Above, it does not yet command from the political agencies the respect and attention of an independent national pressure group. And this is mainly because, below, there is not yet a structure of contact and coalition that would make it such a group.

Mexican-Americans considered for participation on public boards and commissions are judged according to a set of standards which the Anglo does not apply to himself. Some Mexicans are tagged as too middle-class and not grass-roots enough to represent the people in the *barrios*. Other Mexicans are not acceptable because they are presumed to be overidentified with Mexican causes and hence not able to deal with the broad range of groups and problems confronting the decision-makers.

Mexican-Americans are most likely to be chosen to serve on police advisory commissions, welfare advisory councils, and employment advisory committees. Very rarely are they admitted to public utilities or highway commissions, or executive bodies of public commerce, finance, and city planning. Nor do the Mexican-Americans fare much better with respect to public roles in federal agencies. They are more acceptable, it would appear, as the recipients of protection and services than as administrators and technicians. Examples of this are apparent in the Department of Health, Education, and Welfare and the United States Commission on Civil Rights.

COMMUNICATION

Nothing is more striking about the Spanish-speaking communities of the Southwest than the nearly total lack of newspapers and magazines dealing consistently, seriously, and informatively with the special concerns of the minority. There are only two dailies that pretend to even a thin regional circulation—*La Opinion* of Los Angeles and *La Prensa* of San Antonio. Their success is due more to the fact that they are in Spanish than to any enlightenment they spread throughout the *barrios*.

Local weeklies or semi-monthlies crop up and wither away. Some have appeared through the years, intermittently, sustained by heavy advertising during political campaigns. Upon a base of millions of Mexican-Americans in the Southwest no entrepreneur has built a publishing business around which it could be said that a Mexican-American press is forming. Here and there the established English language dailies make amends by publishing an occasional column called "Amigos" or the like. In one large city—Oakland—the only attention that Mexican-American affairs receive is by courtesy of a Negro neighborhood newspaper.

It is to the radio and increasingly to television that the *colonias* turn for common cultural fare. The programs are market-conscious, with much folk music and a little news being the unavoidable fill between the commercials.

There is similarly no interchange of current information and analysis among the community and civic organizations and the most active and alert men and women who spur them. Bulletins and newsletters are issued occasionally, none of them distinguished by comprehensive reporting, scholarly contributions, stimulating controversy, or provocative editorializing.

RESEARCH

The Mexican-Americans have not fared badly in the area of research, if comparison is not made with the sustained support of scholarly work by and about the Negro minority.

Bibliography on the subject of the Mexican-American encompasses the past forty years. Mexican scholars and American professors have paid particular attention to immigration, education, linguistic problems, farm labor, the social anthropology of the *colonia,* and the *bracero.* Religious institutions have published, as byproducts of social service and propagation of their faiths, books and conference reports. The Mexican has had his share of attention in masters' and doctoral theses.

There have been exceptional and authoritative books by Mexican-Americans, but by far the greater part of the bibliography is composed of the work of Anglo students looking in. A recent sampling of 790 published titles of articles, pamphlets, brochures, and an occasional book credited 81 entries to authors with Spanish surnames.

The $400,000 Mexican-American Study project recently completed at the University of California at Los Angeles, financed through a grant of the Ford Foundation, may well be both a capstone for what has preceded in research, and a turning point toward new uses and perhaps even new

methods in this field. One reason for this is that resistance
has set in to the repeated and locally irrelevant incursions
of anthropologists and sociologists into the *barrios*. It is
also true that research has no devices by which its findings
can be given currency and use by the people who are its
subjects.

Further impetus toward a new and broader kind of research is given by the newly-recognized inadequacies of
census counts and other statistical sources of what is called
"impact data." Federal agencies whose programs affect the
Mexican-American community are unable to plan and administer them effectively because they do not have enough
current information. The Department of Health, Education, and Welfare, for instance, has indicated that an intens-
ive nationwide census of the Spanish-speaking population
is necessary before the Department can speak with confidence regarding its problems.

Contributing to this situation is the almost total lack of
historical and literary treatment of the Mexican-American
in the United States. The only threads of fact or fiction to
which the student or scholar may resort are the incidental
romances of the Spanish past or the jolly caricatures of Tor-
tilla Flat. Although literary artists are not made to order,
and the Spanish-speaking people of the Southwest may have
to be patient waiting for them to turn up, the larger society's ways of discovering and encouraging existing talent
must surely be extended to the *barrio* at long last.

4

MINORITY DIVISIONS AND
DILUTION OF POWER

For the overwhelming mass of the Mexican-Americans, life goes on in a culture of poverty. The gross as well as the subtle traits of such a culture are all present, from the high incidence of unemployment to the feelings of distrust toward government and its agencies. This is an American dilemma, second only to that posed by the conditions of black society. It is not only the general society, however, which faces the dilemma. Within the minority there are individuals, still few in number, who have pulled out of the traps of poverty and who now respond to motives other than those that arise from dire necessity. Upon these, a minority within the minority, weigh dilemmas of a personal nature. Entrance into the middle class brings the Mexican-American both material rewards and psychological discomforts. The status attained within the minority cannot easily be swapped for equivalent prestige outside it. If assimilation means total absorption by the dominant culture, which itself remains unchanged, it can lead to uncritical surrender even to those of its elements which produced economic inequalities, racial segregation, and color prejudice in the first place.

It is in this middle area of cultural blur that clichés loosen, making it possible to pursue further definition of the Mexican-American community.

More than four million people concentrated in one region of the country, distinguishable by skin color and using an alien language, give the outward appearance of a solid bloc. This is helpful to census takers, administrators of crash programs with twelve-month deadlines, and persons expected to deliver politically. The concept is of no use to those who are interested in locating the strategic grips for effective action.

The various terms used to identify in one manageable lump the brown human beings who live in the Southwest suggest important differentiations. The Spanish-surnamed include recent immigrants from Mexico, central America, Puerto Rico, and Cuba, as well as the thousands of Filipinos who have made California their home for two generations. The Spanish-Americans of Colorado and New Mexico prefer not to be confused with Mexicans straight out of Sonora. The term Mexican-American breaks in three parts at the hyphen: there are those who regard themselves as "puro Mexicano"; those who consider themselves Americans of Mexican ancestry; and those who feel they are simply Americans of Hispanic lineage. The Spanish language eludes the second and third generations, whose use of their "mother tongue" is confined to a variable mix of isolated words and phrases and highly inventive syntax.

These characteristics represent difficulties of approach to the ethnic minority as a whole because it is not a whole, either as its constituents think of themselves, or as they stratify as aliens and migrants. Distance between these strata within the minority is as important to explain their political powerlessness in the face of the burdens of existence which they bear in common, as the distance between the minority itself and the surrounding society.

Using the term Spanish-surname, those residing in California in 1960 totalled 656,000 persons, of whom 484,000 were of foreign or mixed parentage and 285,000 were foreign born. In Texas the figure was 477,000, with 353,000 of foreign or mixed parentage and 186,000 foreign born.

Citizenship status also cuts across the ethnic bloc. In 1965 approximately 631,000 Mexican aliens registered with the Department of Justice in compliance with legal requirements. Of these 315,000 were in California; 201,000 in Texas; 33,000 in Illinois; 30,000 in Arizona; and 12,000 in New Mexico. These were legally admitted residents. In addition there were in 1965, over 100,000 *braceros* and probably not less than 50,000 illegals. Their separation from the functions of citizenship was total.

No one who has worked in any part of the Southwest as a social worker, community organizer, administrator, teacher, public health officer, or in any other profession charged with providing services in the Mexican-American communities can have missed the effects of this pervading dilution. There is everywhere a large number of politically and culturally immobilized residents. Naturalized Mexicans have relatives or friends in Mexico waiting to follow them. To become a joiner, much less a protester, is to invite "dificultades con las autoridades" that might in some unexplainable way complicate immigration processes. In large cities like Denver the ratio of aliens to others in the minority group may not be higher than two or three out of a hundred; in small *colonias* they can represent 25 to 30 percent of the residents.

The non-citizen, whether he is a registered alien or a *bracero* or an illegal, can be nothing but a petitioner for services. If he has rights recognized by the law, he seeks out intermediaries to plead for him. Even after naturalization, the habit of relying on buffers between oneself and authority persists. This explains why Mexican-American organizations have for decades assumed the enormous task, almost always without charging fees, of mediating services or claiming rights. Oftentimes the only thing requested is information; but considering the number of human beings who ask for it, there is already justification for a publicly funded information and referral agency. Such an agency, in its role of middleman between a socially inchoate class of persons and the assistance they are provided, could never develop either an autonomous economic base or the necessary independence and leverage of respected constituency.

Particularly in the light of current anti-poverty programs it is necessary to try to get down to the real atomic weight of what is called "maximum feasible participation" in minority communities. In the case of the Mexican-Americans some of the subtractions that must be made have been indicated. Another is the large number of youth under eighteen years of age. Still others are the dependents on social assistance, the unemployed, and the aging. These are all political liabilities, in any case, but with the Mexican-American they are compounded by the alienation of language.

The alleged apathy of those surrounded by these difficulties is too easy an answer, and too unenlightening. Apathy is the absence of an expected response. It is supposed to indicate acute mental stasis in the non-respondent. This criticism has been hung on the Mexican-American. But considering the drain on vital energies of unemployment, bad housing, malnutrition, and anxiety, the failure to respond is also a form of self-preservation. The economy of indifference to the abstract, to the seemingly irrelevant, to the repetition of past failures, or to the use of unfamiliar social skills is basically a conserving one.

Disappointment and discouragement are not counteracted by incentives offered in a reverse priority. In the *barrios,* especially in the hard core poverty tracts, the order is jobs, housing, educational opportunity, health services, consumer protection, transportation, and a decent regard for the person. These make up the immediate and concrete elements of community cooperation. After that comes the proper scaling of action so that it is understood and can be managed by its beneficiaries. Finally, there must be attention to the critical details of democratic procedure in meetings, simplicity and directness in the dispatch of business, responsibility in accounting and finances, and the continuing process of teaching and explaining all that goes on. Community action failures among the Mexican-Americans have heightened the distrust and decreased the possibilities of maximum feasible participation.

BLACK AND BROWN AFFINITIES AND FRICTIONS

To intra-minority problems there has been added in the past decade a new stress—the relations of the Mexican and the Negro. In the small towns and the middle-sized cities the two ethnic groups tend to live in isolation from each other. In the large cities black and brown neighborhoods rub elbows. It is not uncommon to find small enclaves of one ringed by solid residential zones of the other, as happens in Los Angeles. Since the educational handicaps of both minorities place them together in the lower economic income levels, their paths cross on the job, in trade unions, in public housing projects, in the public schools, and on the streets. As percentages of the poor, brown and black hold about equal shares of not-having. In the five southwestern states Mexican-Americans and Negroes each account for 17 percent of all poor families.

In the competition for jobs and the bidding for cheap

housing it has generally been the Anglo and Negro who have moved in on the Mexican. The migration of dust bowl whites, and later of blacks, drifted naturally toward farm work and manual labor in the cities, where the Spanish-speaking had already concentrated. There was a time when railway maintenance crews throughout the west, for instance, were preponderantly if not exclusively composed of brown-skinned men. In agriculture in the 1940's the domination of harvest labor by Mexicans was reduced by white and Negro migrants until all three were severely shaken by the *braceros.*

During the last ten years these forms of competition have become more severe, reflecting the sharp pinch of unemployment on Negroes and Mexicans alike. Where the two minorities are numerous the highest rates of unemployment for both are found. But, though it is not likely to diminish, job competition by itself does not bode open conflict between the two races. Relations between the two groups are remarkably free of organized aggression.

However, the accommodation that has existed at the low income levels, is by no means guaranteed to last, for there are, in addition to job competition, other points of friction. Negro and Mexican politicians are competing for the small portion of public power allowed them by the white establishment. The distribution of anti-poverty funds created a kind of watchful jealousy on both sides. In trade unions with considerable black and brown membership, blocs have formed, each with an eye on key staff positions and the control of job assignments.

Additionally, the Mexican-American community has been stirred by the civil rights movement, and the resulting division of opinions would indicate that in this area even a small measure of acculturation has brought its penalties with its rewards. Among some Mexican-Americans there is a latent hostility against the Negro that is not based on economic pressures. It is certainly not indigenous to the culture of poverty among Mexicans, but abetted, if it does not indeed stem from, their uncritical acceptance of American middle class racial contagion. The rumbles of a gang fight can intensify the growing uneasiness. Sporadic efforts have been made to give the Negro token support in his civil rights demonstrations; they represent the convictions of a few, not a groundswell of sympathetic opinion.

This is understandable. The Mexican-American has had his share of discrimination and segregation, but the Southwest has never been the Deep South. The centuries of brutal social affronts that humiliated equally the Negro sharecropper, the Negro businessman, the Negro laborer and the Negro intellectual, solidifying them emotionally if not tactically, were the mainspring of their current revolt. In Mexican-American society this has not been so. No overwhelming and collective revulsion against the Anglo exists that would mass all brown men against him, much less rally them all in support of the Negro. The new militancy of the young, while rousing Mexican-Americans generally to basic and long-standing inequalities in the "system," does not and probably never will have the unanimous support of the Mexican-American community.

The recency of the mixing of Negroes and Mexicans in the Southwest; the participation of the Negro at least in the formal processes of government that the Mexican-American has been able to see for himself; indeed, the superior organizing experience and the local political successes of the black man explain why the *barrios* have not pitched into the civil rights battle. Had the gross evils of segregation and discrimination existed in the Southwest as they did in the Deep South, they would probably have been visited upon the brown men also as the joint tenants of economic exploitation. These historical conditions for solidarity do not exist. This is not to shrug off the fact that a latent hostility against the Anglo does exist. It, too, has erupted, as it did in the Los Angeles "zoot-suit riots."*

As the Negro is not marking time in his successes and his defeats, neither is the Mexican-American resting easily on his comparative luck. A single lesson appears to be in the making for both the black man and the brown. The deprivation of economic and educational opportunity is about equal for both—equally crippling. But they appraise this common lot from different angles, each rooted in the particular historical experience. The Negro regards the establishment of his moral and spiritual worth as a prerequisite of economic progress; the Mexican has not, until very recently, considered this necessary. When the two minorities begin to move with the same determination toward full economic citizenship, the Mexican-American will be found to be a responsive ally, provided the Negro does not allow the ambiguities of black power, as the Mexican-Americans see them, to become an insurmountable barrier.

Useful insights into the future concerning this important alliance are part of the pending business before the Mexican-American. Clues to some of them may perhaps be discovered through a closer look at the institutional relations between American society and this minority.

---

*In June 1943, American sailors and other servicemen stationed in the Los Angeles area "invaded" Mexican-American neighborhoods, notably the populous *barrio* of East Los Angeles. After clashing with another group of sailors on leave, the mob vented its hostility on brown-skinned "zoot suiters." Newspaper headlines, reflecting the bias of an unfriendly press, gave these events the typically inaccurate description of "zoot suit riots."

5

THE "ANGLO" AND THE
MEXICAN-AMERICAN

During the first two or three decades of large-scale emigration and the settlement of the first *colonias* it may be said that the Mexican was regarded almost solely as an economic input in the building of the Southwest. Business enterprise was the only connection he had to the established Anglo society (the term "Anglo" covers the entire non-Mexican spectrum, inaccurately, if less abrasively than the pungent "gringo"). Where he lived, whether or not his children attended school, the adequacy of his pay, the availability or lack of health services, the ways in which he could survive seasonal unemployment were not, in the early years, the formal concern of the society that used him. If he and his family went hungry or shivered in unheatable shacks, these were private hardships suffered unobtrusively.

Inevitably, these strangers were reached by another type of Anglo, the volunteer helper who saw them through the eyes of American morality. These were the teachers, priests, ministers, social workers, professors, and civil servants who noted the accumulating deprivation of the Mexican slums, taught the children, and showed respect for their parents' culture. Through their churches, their homes, their schoolrooms, their charities, and their warmth they provided the first experiences beyond those of hard work and meager living.

As long as migration was light the social helpers could cope to a degree with the integration of the new minority. But as they increased, the Mexican-Americans compelled the attention of the institutions and agencies of government. They crowded into the schools of certain neighborhoods. They hungered through the winters. They queued in the county hospitals. To their needs were added, in the 1930's, those of a tide of migrants from the white and black south. Together they became the objects of the social legislation that ensued. Paralleling public assistance, private services reached out to ever-increasing numbers of dependents. The agency became the primary medium of social service, the front line of contact between the minority and the host society.

On both sides of that line significant adaptations took place. In the agencies the bureaucracy grew. Complexity set in. A new vocabulary appeared. Professionalism created levels of diminishing touch and increasing distance between the givers and the receivers.

Within the *barrios* the adaptations made necessary by the inescapable contact with this apparatus were gradually invented. The few who knew a little more English and had learned the ways of the agencies became the busy and unpaid indigenous aides of the neighborhood. Barbers gave advice on how to file a wage claim, bartenders on industrial accident procedure, grocers on time-payment contracts. These services were professionalized when a second generation of Mexican-American attorneys, brokers, accountants, teachers, and doctors emerged.

It is at this stage that the Mexican-American community now finds itself, and its essential function may be described as that of a switchboard through which flows the traffic of information, interpretation, delivery and receipt of services, grievances, and compliance. All this requires a very considerable body of full-time civil servants in the agencies and of small entrepreneurs and volunteers in the *barrios*. Together they render what is basically a technical service, a refinement of the technics of dependency.

Since 1964, however, the Economic Opportunity Act and the programs arising from it have had two effects: they have posed an alternative to dependency; and they have sharpened attention on the ways in which agency-community relations have helped to perpetuate dependency.

At the outset, the new programs created obvious needs for the agencies, particularly those receiving federal assistance. The agencies required dependable profiles of sprawling ghettos and the compacted poverty tracts within them. They had to discover ways to penetrate these communities through channels of communication that could be kept reasonably free of misinformation and irrelevancies. They needed direct connection with local leaders and, having found them, tactful guidance on how to avoid the frictions between them. They sought candidates with bilingual skills for appointment to staff positions. Not infrequently they were pressed to find cases and grievances for which the law provided funds and remedies, always keeping in mind that future appropriations depended on present performance.

A standard approach to the Mexican-American minority soon developed. Each agency worked its way through the same perplexities, shooting at the "target area" from its own quiver. All of them competed for the same limited number of potential candidates for staff positions. Each one concentrated on highly particular definitions of individual and community. To each the Spanish-speaking minority in a county or a metropolis continued to look like an undifferentiated demographic clump resistant to services, even those promoted with the grimmest devotion.

Of course, some of these services, such as consumer protection, merely bounced off the surface of the clump. Others, like juvenile control, which could count on police power, established their iron roots in the *barrios*. In between, educational counseling and mental health programs experimented hopefully and hesitated timidly between causes and symptoms. Some forms of assistance were totally ignored, such as the provision of unemployment clinics where adult workers out of jobs might have learned what neither the schools nor the trade unions were teaching them.

Every important problem of the *barrios* is the product of a historical process. The solution of those problems requires historical perspective into the future as well as into the past. But agency programs dealing with housing, fair hiring practices, education, and employment have become typical of federally financed programs: they expand or contract, often drastically, within the cycle of the fiscal year. Thus subject to bureaucratic manipulation, program structure can easily be abused. Directly affected by these fluctuations is the community's own self-help structure through which collective life is held together, tentatively, experimentally, often anxiously, but always tending to produce patterns of behavior which are concrete, immediate, and trusted. The necessary condition for the working out of those patterns is a degree of permanence and stability. To its traumatic encounters with economic dislocation and demographic shocks, the Mexican-American *barrio* now had to add the changes of pace and of direction of fiscal year budgeting.

The Mexican-American community has also been making the discovery, in bewilderment and disappointment, that a middle layer of political power can intervene between itself and the best intentions of federal programs. This middle layer is composed of the bureaucratic networks of state and particularly local government that are close at hand and avowedly ready to carry out those programs. When these networks are in the hands of powers whose base is distant from or indifferent or even hostile to the minority, they can hobble those programs, or even reject them. For there is one thing which the federal agencies of the welfare state may not attempt, and that is to create constituencies that will support them politically and legislatively, as the constituencies of the military and defense agencies do. These realities were implied in a recent statement of one federal administrator who noted that even where large numbers of Mexican-Americans are present in a community it cannot be assumed that the local public school is serving their interests or meeting their needs. Access to the resource bank of public services is not guaranteed by congressional enactment. It is not yet very clear to the Mexican-American community why this is so. Its perplexity has been increased by its experience with anti-poverty programs.

The highlights of this experience deserve attention. Two very disparate elements were brought into the hastily organized partnership of the community action agencies. One was the combination of established agencies of public and private philanthropy, with their sophistication, resources, seasoned know-how, and well ordered chains of command. The other was the primitive organization of the poor. Unlike the agency representatives with whom they were teamed on the commissions and boards that became the local arms of the Office of Economic Opportunity, the elected or designated spokesmen of the poverty tracts came to their task with no sub-systems of influence, much less of power, behind them. The vacuum was filled instantly by officers and employees of the established agencies and institutions, and by the thin upper layer of the minority middle class who kept their ties with the poor from a variety of motives, noble or self-serving. The Economic Opportunity Act, at Title II, contained profound implications for the nation. The time would be short until those implications would become clear to its opponents. When their reaction set in the established agencies had no need to defend the OEO with their bureaucratic lives. For them the business of dependency could still go on in the old ways. For the middle class the choice was either to recognize their weaknesses and set about curing them, or to plunge into the competition for the funds offered by the Act.

The latter course prevailed and the poor again lost out on any real reform. The programs presented on their behalf by newborn poverty foundations and non-profit corporations were inevitably patterned on those of the agencies. They were for direct individual services. They required immediately a bureaucracy. Power was not diffused. Policy was pyramided. Funds for administration had the priority. Originality and innovation in programming stopped halfway between the prepackaged assignments issued by Washington and the stirring resentment, the organizational confusion of the poverty tracts.

The principle of pressure spending operated on the unbalanced community-action bodies and in the competition for funds. Every twelve months the federal till had to be cleaned out in preparation for the fiscal year refill. Funding and refunding became the central technical problems, not the organizational defects of community action programs and the inchoate mass of clients beyond them. The inclination to use finances in a hurry because Congress had appropriated them appeared at times to be a strong incentive of programming. To spend money because it is there is, from a functional point of view, as much of a weakness as not spending it because it is *not* there, need being established.

The OEO program was routed off the main line to other side tracks. Representatives of the poor allowed themselves to sit as referees with screening powers over their peers, thus tacitly endorsing the distribution of the little that the congressional appropriations allowed. Area or county-wide program packaging tended to imitate locally the federal prototype. There was a swift preemption of those who had any experience in community organization, moving them downtown and upstairs in a heady bureaucratic climb.

By the fall of 1966, with hardly three years of combat behind it, the war on poverty in the Mexican-American *colonias* was showing heavy casualties. In the end, it was still not the errors of strategy or the problems of tactics that commanded the attention of the disappointed, but the bickering over administrative maneuvers.

The experience has been instructive, however, and some Mexican-Americans are beginning to take their own reading of its lessons. The ingrained habit of self-help has moved one step closer to systematic and stable forms of community cooperation. Seriously considered for the first time is the idea that these forms are capable of democratic control that will reduce, perhaps eliminate, dependency. The word "corporation" has recovered, as a synonym of joint action, a dim connotation of community. The right of representation has now been vaguely but vitally connected with the concept of economic opportunity. On the threshhold of the practical application of these lessons and the resolution of the many problems that still bar their realization, the Mexican-American minority does indeed begin to move into the mainstream of American life. It is not yet the swift midcurrent of success and its goods, only the rational formulation of a choice between the meaningless accumulation of material wealth and other possibilities. Brown men or black, if they are capable of such choices, they are no longer "minors," no matter how few their numbers.

6

THE FUTURE

A minority is almost by definition a problem as viewed from the outside by the general society. The present generation of Mexican-Americans, as an ethnic group, carries the stigma of dependency, which means inadequacy, which implies non-competency, which by degrees leads to the second sense of the word "minority." Minors are persons who have to be dealt with through practical combinations of tolerance, forbearance, persuasion, oversight, firmness, and occasionally force. Minors who number millions and who have grown to adulthood without achieving independence are costly. The deprivations they suffer must be mitigated at the expense of others.

Minority problems have been avoided or abolished by prohibition of immigration, by assimilation, and even by extermination. The last solution is not known to be under consideration for the Mexican-American. The second is working by slow degrees from one generation to the next, slowed down by what amounts, in practice, to a rejection of the first. The Mexican-American problem, for those who choose to think of it that way, will endure.

This is a predominantly young demographic group. It is likely to sustain the present high rate of reproduction during the next two or three decades, now twice that of the general society. Immigration, at the present pace, will add 40,000 or more newcomers each year. By the end of 1970 it is likely that in the Southwest the total population of the Spanish - speaking, the Spanish - surnamed, the Mexican-Americans—whatever their designation—will be well over 5 million, and possibly closer to 6 million.

These will be predominantly, one could say overwhelmingly, poor people. Although the Mexican economy is spinning at a high rate of growth it also shows a chronic incapacity to distribute more evenly the new wealth. Those who are able to cross the border into the United States will gravitate toward the hard-core poverty tracts in which the language, the customs and the privation will be familiar. The Mexican-American *barrios* will continue to be concentrations of poor people. These will be urban concentrations. In the central cities, where planners are busy, the dislocation of the *barrios* that presently have the greatest absorbing capacity will certainly continue.

For the new migrants the problem of making a living will depend upon whether there is an upward movement of their predecessors which would vacate manual jobs. The forecast in this direction is not encouraging, to put it mildly. There is no prospect of a grand breakthrough in educational and vocational opportunity.

If risks are to be taken in prophecy it would be safer to take them on the side of the probability that the cost of social assistance to the Mexican-Americans will rise rather than fall at present standards of need and levels of welfare expenditure. The *colonia,* for all its capacity to share its scarcities of housing, food, and employment, has no visible savings or institutions to encourage enterprise or extend charity. Help must continue to come from the outside, and it must be aimed primarily at the Mexican family, under siege by the increasing pressures of urban existence which make even more difficult parental control and protection against the particular stresses of the *barrio*. If the cost of helping these families is high, the alternative—banishing Mexican dependency to Mexico, as was done thirty years ago when unemployed Mexicans by the thousands were deported—would be even more expensive in terms of international opinion.

As an urban dweller by the hundreds of thousands, the Mexican-American will continue to live in or close to the Negro pockets of poverty. If the minorities are pitted against each other, each will be aroused by self-preservation. If they are moved by cooperation, they may yet make common cause.

7

A SUMMARY

The following is a recapitulation of findings about the economic, cultural, political, and educational condition of Mexican-Americans in the Southwest as presented in the preceding chapters of this book.

• From one third to one half of the Mexican-Americans in this region live below the official level of poverty or immediately above it.

• They are predominantly manual workers and thus locked within the lowest brackets of wage income.

• The dwellings of the many are located in deteriorated rural and urban tracts, and those of the few in middle-class neighborhoods.

• Because of their economic status they bear the greatest impact of mechanization and automation.

• Educational opportunity has been denied them to the extent that as an ethnic group they trail by three to four years or more the attainments of the general society.

• They are now more than 80 percent urbanized.

• Concentration in the city and the metropolis has produced massive clusters of population with satellites of smaller rural settlements.

• In each of these clusters there are important differences in economic activity and cultural self-identification.

• With these differences in mind the Mexican-American southwesterners may not be regarded as a bloc, but rather as a demographic aggregation differentiated within by citizenship status and the distance in time from the ancestral Mexican culture.

• The shorter this distance the more the Spanish language operates as a binder within the community and as a barrier outside it.

• Mobility of the Mexican-American masses is now primarily the result of shifts upward in the technological qualifications for jobs and urban removal caused by urban renewal.

• For a defense against the adverse effects of these changes the Mexican-American does not yet have an organization capable of informing and mobilizing him even within the area clusters, much less within the region.*

• In a way that is entirely peculiar to national origin and geographic location, the Mexican-American condition reflects the pressures of population within Mexico and along the border, and the international relations between Mexico and the United States regarding immigration, trade, and investment.

• In order to deal with the effects of economic and cultural deprivation the Mexican-American minority has tried persistently to organize itself.

• In the course of these efforts a certain range of goals and modes of action have emerged, including the direct service programs of local volunteer groups, quasi-political

---

*The Southwest Council of La Raza, a regional organization with potential national impact, was established as a direct result of this study. Funded by the Ford Foundation, the organization presents a broad-front approach to the problems confronting Mexican-Americans and places particular emphasis on recruiting and working at the *barrio* level.

and civic action organizations with state and regional affiliates, professional fraternities and intellectual cadres.

 • The effectiveness of these neighborhood community groups has been hampered by the excessive burdens on a few and the lack of resources.

 • Failure of the groups is caused by a lack of both technical assistance and basic organizational resources.

 • Individuals with private wealth within the minority have shown little concern for the aspirations of the community, and outside it private philanthropy has taken little notice.

 • The expansion of agency social programs, mainly under federal legislation, has, while opening new careers for the indigenous volunteers, enticed them from their original community base.

 • Communications between agency and client have improved with the models of bureaucratic organization and devices of action offered by those programs, and have remained almost non-existent between the groups within the minority.

 • The imitation of these models under the haste and stress of the anti-poverty program has brought disappointments and miscarriages, the effects of which are already felt but not yet fully understood.

 • At the sensitive points of informed discussion and analysis the Mexican-American apprehends a new and hazardous role of critic instead of broker or mere beneficiary.

 • Henceforth this role will include unavoidably the central issues of economic opportunity and civil equality.

APPENDIX

Spanish-surname population in the five southwestern states of California, Texas, Colorado, New Mexico and Arizona — 1960.

Arizona	194,356
California	1,426,538
Colorado	157,173
New Mexico	269,122
Texas	1,417,810

Source: U.S. Census 1960.

Percentage growth of Spanish-surname population in the five southwestern states — 1950 to 1960.

Arizona	51.4
California	87.6
Colorado	33.0
New Mexico	8.1
Texas	37.1

Source: U.S. Census 1950, 1960.

Distribution of Spanish-surname population of Mexican stock* by selected states — 1960.

California	695,643
Indiana	14,041
Arizona	105,342
Illinois	63,063
New Mexico	34,559
Michigan	24,298
Colorado	20,091
Indiana	14,041
Washington	11,084
New York	10,074

*A person born in Mexico or having at least one Mexican-born parent.

Source: U.S. Census 1960.

Distribution in the Southwest of Spanish-surname population of United States-born Mexican stock* — 1960.

Total (5 states)	1,899,402
Texas	776,284
California	656,674
New Mexico	235,342
Colorado	135,277
Arizona	95,825

Source: U.S. Census 1960.

*A U.S. native of Mexican ancestry both of whose parents were born in the United States.

Spanish-surname population in selected standard metropolitan areas in the five southwestern states, and percentage of total population — 1960.

	SPANISH-SURNAME POPULATION	PERCENT OF TOTAL
ARIZONA		
Phoenix	78,996	11.9
Tucson	44,481	16.7
CALIFORNIA		
Fresno	61,418	16.8
Los Angeles - Long Beach	629,292	9.3
San Diego	64,810	6.3
San Francisco - Oakland	177,239	6.4
San Jose	77,755	12.1
Stockton	30,585	12.2
COLORADO		
Denver	60,294	6.5
Pueblo	25,437	21.4
Colorado Springs	6,135	4.3
NEW MEXICO		
Albuquerque	68,101	26.0
TEXAS		
Austin	26,072	12.3
Brownsville - Harlingen - San Benito	96,744	64.0
El Paso	136,993	43.6
Laredo	257,090	37.4

Source: U.S. Census 1960.

Concentration of Spanish-surname population in selected counties in Arizona, California and Texas — 1960.

ARIZONA

Ten largest counties	187,000
Maricopa	79,000
Pima	44,000

CALIFORNIA

Ten largest counties	773,000
Los Angeles	576,000
San Francisco Bay area	145,000

TEXAS

Ten largest counties	912,000
Bexar	257,000
El Paso	136,000
Hidalgo	129,000

Source: U.S. Census 1960.

Distribution of Spanish-surname population by selected counties in California — 1960.

Total (58 counties)	1,426,538
Los Angeles	576,000
Santa Clara	77,755
Alameda	67,866
San Diego	64,810
Fresno	61,418
San Bernardino	60,177
Orange	52,576
San Francisco	51,602
Riverside	36,224
Ventura	33,980
San Joaquin	30,585
Sacramento	30,078

Source: U.S. Census 1960.

Distribution by age of Spanish-surname persons in Los Angeles County — 1960.

AGE GROUP	NUMBER	PER-CENT
0 to 4 years	90,449	15.7
5 to 14	133,861	23.2
15 to 19	44,985	7.8
20 to 24	41,493	7.2
25 to 54	213,010	36.9
55 to 64	30,953	5.4
65 and over	21,965	3.8

Source: U.S. Census 1960.

Distribution of Spanish-surname population by selected counties in Colorado — 1960.

Total (63 counties)	157,000
Denver	43,147
Pueblo	25,437
Weld	8,831
Alamosa	8,542
Las Animas	7,443
Fremont	6,135
Otero	5,328
Conejos	4,476

Source: The Status of Spanish-surnamed Citizens in Colorado. Based on U.S. Census 1960.

Distribution by age group of Spanish-surname population in
Colorado — 1960.

	PERCENT
Under 5 years	11.98
5 to 9 years	12.14
10 to 14	12.35
15 to 19	11.55
20 to 24	9.87
25 to 29	9.07
30 to 34	8.51
35 to 39	7.08
40 to 44	6.08
45 to 49	6.14
50 to 54	6.11
55 to 59	5.86
60 to 64	5.36
65 and over	4.61

Source: The Status of Spanish-surnamed Citizens in Colorado.
Based on U.S. Census 1960.

Spanish-surname civilian labor force in the five southwestern
states — 1960.

	MALE	FEMALE
Total civilian labor force	801,045	285,417
Number unemployed	64,277	28,512
Percent unemployed	8.0	8.6

Source: U.S. Census 1960.

Concentration of employed urban Spanish-surname males in the five southwestern states — 1960.

	PERCENT
Professional	.34
Managers and proprietors	.38
Clerical	.75
Sales	.50
Craft	.90
Operative	1.50
Private household	.82
Service (non-private)	1.24
Laborer	2.37
Farm labor	5.24

Source: U.S. Census 1960.

Industry distribution of employed Spanish-surname persons fourteen years old and over in California — 1960.

Agriculture, forestry and fisheries	68,683
Mining	1,088
Construction	31,077
Manufacturing	135,885
Transportation	28,857
Wholesale and retail trade	73,001
Finance, insurance, real estate	12,061
Business and repair services	11,886
Personal services	24,106
Entertainment and recreation	4,945
Professional and related services	24,986
Public administration	16,914

Source: U.S. Census 1960.

Family income in 1959 of Spanish-surname heads of urban
and rural households in the five southwestern states.

URBAN FAMILIES

Total	567,000
Under $3,000	175,000
Under $1,000	43,000
$1,000 to $2,999	132,000
$3,000 and over	393,000

RURAL FAMILIES

Total	131,000
Under $3,000	68,000
Under $1,000	18,000
$1,000 to $2,999	50,000
$3,000 and over	63,000

Source: U.S. Census 1960.

Number of Texas migrants working in selected states in 1964.
(A total of 37 states employed Texas migrants in 1964.)

Michigan	28,598
Ohio	21,921
Wisconsin	17,982
Idaho	15,709
Illinois	14,841
Indiana	13,354
Minnesota	10,427
Oregon	6,343
Colorado	5,674
Montana	5,265
Washington	4,338
Wyoming	3,974
Nebraska	3,345

SOURCE: Julian Samora (ed.), *La Raza: Forgotten Americans* (Notre
Dame, Ind.: University of Notre Dame Press, 1966).

Educational attainment in percentages of Spanish-surname persons in the five southwestern states — 1960.

	AGE 14–24	AGE 25 AND OVER
0 – 4 years	9.0	35.6
8 years	16.3	11.5
12 years	14.0	12.2
Some college	4.2	6.2

Source: Joan W. Moore, *Mexican-Americans: Problems and Prospects* (Madison, Wisc.: Institute for Research on Poverty, 1968).

Spanish-surname enrollments as percentage of all enrollments in public schools in selected California counties—1966.

San Benito	51.12
Imperial	44.31
Fresno	28.15
Madera	27.92
Tulare	27.37
Kings	21.97
Monterey	18.30
Merced	18.17
Riverside	17.25
Ventura	16.50
Santa Barbara	16.35
Los Angeles	15.61
Santa Clara	15.52
San Francisco	12.19
San Diego	10.59

Source: Racial and ethnic survey of California public schools, 1966.

Educational achievement of Spanish-surname persons age 25 years and over in Los Angeles County — 1960.

TOTAL NUMBER OF PERSONS: 265,928 YEARS OF SCHOOL	PERCENT OF TOTAL
None	7.0
1 – 7	30.0
8 – 11	37.0
12	17.5
13 – 15	5.9
16 or more	3.0

MEDIAN SCHOOL YEARS COMPLETED: 9

Source: U.S. Census 1960.

Educational achievement of Spanish-surname persons age 25 years and over in New Mexico — 1960.

YEARS OF SCHOOL	NUMBER OF PERSONS	PERCENT OF TOTAL
1 – 4	21,761	20.3
5 – 7	24,362	22.7
8	15,181	14.2
9 – 11	15,622	14.6
12	13,338	12.4
13 – 15	3,899	3.6
16 or more	3,068	2.9

Source: Minority Groups in New Mexico. Based on U.S. Census 1960.

Mexican citizens admitted as contract workers for temporary employment in U.S. agriculture — 1957 to 1967.

1957	436,049
1958	432,857
1959	437,643
1960	315,846
1961	291,420
1962	194,978
1963	186,865
1964	177,736
1965	20,284
1966	7,647
1967	6,125

Source: *Texas Migrant Labor* (Texas Good Neighbor Commission, 1968).

Number of Mexican immigrants to the United States by five year periods — 1900 to 1964.

1900 – 1904	2,259
1905 – 1909	21,732
1910 – 1914	82,588
1915 – 1919	91,075
1920 – 1924	249,248
1925 – 1929	238,527
1930 – 1934	19,200
1935 – 1939	8,737
1940 – 1944	16,548
1945 – 1949	37,742
1950 – 1954	78,723
1955 – 1959	214,746
1960 – 1964	217,827

Source: Joan W. Moore, *Mexican-Americans: Problems and Prospects* (Madison, Wisc.: Institute for Research on Poverty, 1968).

Population of principal Mexican border cities — 1960.

Ciudad Juarez 309,337
Mexicali 277,302
Tijuana 166,572
Matamoros 139,397
Reinosa 133,852
Nogales 39,708
Nuevo Laredo 93,295
Piedras Negras 45,295

Source: Antonio Bermudez, *Defensa fronteriza.*